AEROFILMS GUIDE

# FOOTBALL
# GROUNDS

## ELEVENTH REVISED EDITION

# AEROFILMS GUIDE
# FOOTBALL GROUNDS
## ELEVENTH REVISED EDITION

Ian Allan
PUBLISHING

# CONTENTS

## CONTENTS

*Front cover:* **Despite a somewhat traumatic season in the club's first campaign at the Walkers Stadium, Leicester City succeeded in obtaining automatic promotion, thus ensuring that Premiership fans will have two new grounds to visit in 2003/04.**

*Back cover:* **Following the triumph of the 2002 Commonwealth Games, the stadium constructed for the Games was completed with the construction of the fourth side and, as intended, will form the home of Manchester City from the start of the 2003/04 season.**

*Preceding pages:* **The success of the new Kingston Communications Stadium in Hull has shown the potential of the city as a footballing centre, with the team attracting much larger crowds than in previous seasons. The ground is perhaps one of the more spectacular to have been constructed for a team outside the Premiership and has the scope for further expansion if the club's ambitions can match the city's. Elsewhere, the long drawn out saga of Wembley was finally concluded in the summer with work on the demolition of the old ground concluded by the winter; work has now begun on the replacement with an anticipated completion date of 2006.**

First published in 1993;
Reprinted 1993 (twice); Second edition 1994; Third edition 1995; Fourth edition 1996; Fifth edition 1997; Sixth edition 1998; Seventh edition 1999; Eighth edition 2000; Ninth edition 2001; tenth edition 2002; 11th edition 2003, reprinted 2003.

ISBN 0 7110 2961 X

Published by Ian Allan Publishing
an imprint of Ian Allan Publishing Ltd, Hersham, Surrey KT12 4RG.
Printed by Ian Allan Printing Ltd, Hersham, Surrey KT12 4RG.

Code: 0308/E2

Text © Ian Allan Publishing Ltd 1993-2003
Diagrams © Ian Allan Publishing Ltd 2000-3
Aerial Photography © Aerofilms

Aerofilms Limited have been specialists in aerial photography since 1919. Their library of aerial photographs, both new and old, is in excess of 1.5 million images. Aerofilms undertake to commission oblique and vertical survey aerial photography, which is processed and printed in their specialised photographic laboratory. Digital photomaps are prepared using precision scanners.

Free photostatic proofs are available on request for any site held within the collection and price lists will be forwarded detailing the size of photographic enlargement available without any obligation to purchase.

# Introduction

This is the 11th edition of the *Aerofilms Guide: Football Grounds* and, as usual, the book has been fully updated to take account of the changes to the composition of the FA Premiership and Football League for the start of the 2003/04 season.

In the period since this book was first published, football has witnessed a considerable revolution both in the facilities provided for supporters — witness the fact that almost a quarter of clubs now play at new grounds and that many others have seen considerable investment in upgraded facilities — and in the money that the game generates. The summer of 2002, just as the 10th edition of this guide was being prepared, saw the first sign of harsh economic reality descending on the game with the demise of ITV Digital. In the 12 months since then, many clubs within the Football League have struggled to make ends meet and a number of high profile teams have been forced to go into Administration as efforts are made to regularise their position. Currently, a number of teams are in financial crisis; indeed, a number of teams listed in this guide are by no means certain to survive to start the 2003/04 season. The FA is already starting the negotiations for the new television contract for the Premiership and every indication is that the money coming into the top teams will be lower than under the current deal. What the consequences of this will be is unclear, but it is certainly true that a number of top teams are already facing a financial pinch.

Despite the off-the-field financial problems, football itself remains an ever-increasingly popular spectator, with attendances reaching levels not previously seen for two generations. Thus the imperative to increase ground capacities and improve facilities will continue, but perhaps will be tempered by the financial constraints outlined above. At least one of the teams to go into Administration was brought to the point of collapse by its huge investment in an improved ground and both clubs and financial institutions will be less willing to invest if the risk cannot be properly managed.

For this new edition, we welcome back to the Football League one of the traditional names from the past — Doncaster Rovers — and a new name — Yeovil Town — as a result of the policy of promoting two from the Conference. Elsewhere, new grounds for Darlington (finally?), Manchester City, Hull City and Wimbledon (possibly — will the saga ever end?) are also featured.

As always, may we take this opportunity of wishing you and your team a successful campaign in 2003/04.

## Disabled Facilities

We endeavour to list the facilities for disabled spectators at each ground. Readers will appreciate that these facilities can vary in number and quality and that, for most clubs, pre-booking is essential. Some clubs also have dedicated parking for disabled spectators; this again should be pre-booked if available.

# MILLENNIUM STADIUM

## Westgate Street, Cardiff CF10 1JA

**Tel No:** 029 2023 2661
**Fax:** 029 2023 2678
**Stadium Tours:** 02920 822228
**Web Site:** www.millenniumstadium-sportcentric.com
**Brief History:** The stadium, built upon the site of the much-loved and historic Cardiff Arms Park, was opened in 2000 and cost in excess of £100 million (a tiny sum in comparison with the current forecast spend — if it happens — of over £600 million on the redevelopment of Wembley). As the national stadium for Wales, the ground will be primarily used in sporting terms by Rugby Union, but will be used by the FA to host major fixtures (such as FA Cup and Worthington Cup finals) until, in theory,

2004 when the new Wembley was scheduled for completion.
**(Total) Current Capacity:** 72,500
**Nearest Railway Station:** Cardiff Central
**Parking (Car):** Street parking only.
**Parking (Coach/Bus):** As directed by the police
**Police Force and Tel No:** South Wales (029 2022 2111)
**Disabled Visitors' Facilities:**
　**Wheelchairs:** c250 designated seats. The whole stadium has been designed for ease of disabled access with lifts, etc.
　**Blind:** Commentary available.
**Anticipated Development(s):** None planned

*KEY*

⬆ North direction (approx)

❶ Cardiff Central station
❷ Bus station
❸ River Taff
❹ Castle Street
❺ Westgate Street
❻ Wood Street
❼ Tudor Street
❽ High Street
❾ St Mary Street
❿ To Cardiff Queen Street station

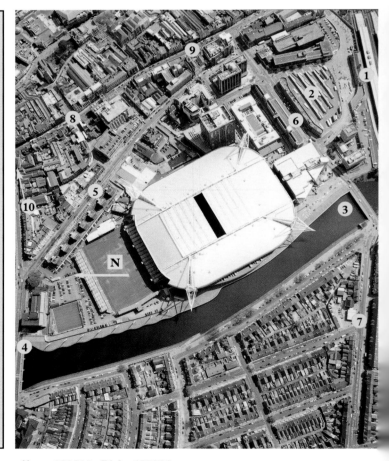

*Above: 688019; Right: 687998*

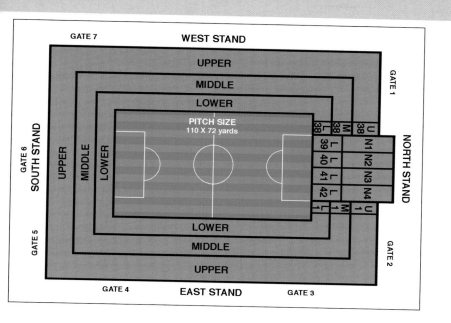

GATE 7

**WEST STAND**

GATE 1

UPPER

MIDDLE

LOWER

**PITCH SIZE**
110 X 72 yards

| U 38 | M 38 | L 38 |
| N1 | L 38 | 39 |
| N2 | L | 40 |
| N3 | L | 41 |
| N4 | L | 42 |
| U 1 | M 1 | L 1 |

**NORTH STAND**

GATE 6

**SOUTH STAND**

UPPER

MIDDLE

LOWER

LOWER

MIDDLE

UPPER

GATE 5

GATE 2

GATE 4

**EAST STAND**

GATE 3

# ARSENAL

## Arsenal Stadium, Avenell Road, Highbury, London, N5 1BU

**Tel No:** 020 7704 4000
**Advance Tickets Tel No:** 020 7704 4040
**Fax:** 020 7704 4001
**Web Site:** www.arsenal.com
**E-Mail:** info@arsenal.co.uk
**League:** F.A. Premier
**Brief History:** Founded 1886 as Royal Arsenal, changed to Woolwich Arsenal in 1891, and Arsenal in 1914. Former grounds: Plumstead Common, Sportsman Ground, Manor Ground (twice), moved to Arsenal Stadium (Highbury) in 1913. Record attendance 73,295
**(Total) Current Capacity:** 38,548 (all seated)
**Visiting Supporters' Allocation:** 2,900 (all seated Clock End and Lower Tier West Stand)
**Club Colours:** Red shirts with white sleeves, white shorts
**Nearest Railway Station:** Drayton Park or Finsbury Park (main line). Arsenal (tube)

**Parking (Car):** Street Parking
**Parking (Coach/Bus):** Drayton Park
**Police Force and Tel No:** Metropolitan (020 7263 9090)
**Disabled Visitors' Facilities:**
  **Wheelchairs:** Lower tier East Stand
  **Blind:** Commentary available
**Anticipated Development(s):** In the middle of April the club issued a statement relating to the development of the new ground at Ashburton Grove. It stated that, whilst the club remained committed to the construction of the new 60,000-seat ground, the complexity of the project meant that it was unable to open the new stadium for the start of the 2005/06 season as planned. Clearly the complexity (and cost) of the £400 million project is one factor in the delay and so expect the Gunners to be based at Highbury for at least the next two seasons plus.

### KEY

**C** Club Offices
**S** Club Shop
**E** Entrance(s) for visiting supporters

↑ North direction (approx)

❶ Avenell Road
❷ Highbury Hill
❸ Gillespie Road
❹ To Drayton Park BR Station (¼ mile)
❺ Arsenal Tube Station
❻ Clock End
❼ St Thomas's Road (to Finsbury Park station)
❽ North Bank
❾ West Stand
❿ East Stand

*Above:* 688318; *Right:* 688311

ollowing the triumph of the double at the end of the 2001/02 season, there was talk that the balance
 power in English football had shifted away from Manchester and was to be found now at Highbury
 d, for much of the season, that certainly seemed to be the case, as the Gunners marched towards the
 A Cup final and took a multi-point lead in the Premiership. However, a drop in form towards the end
 the season, combined with injuries and suspensions, saw the Championship migrate back to Old
 afford and Wenger's team fail to proceed beyond the second group stage in the Champions League.
 he one bright spot was the club's success in the FA Cup, where the Gunners became the first club for
 ore than 20 years successfully to defend the title. A 1-0 victory over Southampton at the Millennium
 adium ensured that some silverware will be added to the Highbury trophy room although the match
could well have marked the end
of an era with a number of
senior players possibly playing
for the team for the last time.

UPPER
WEST STAND
LOWER
AWAY

PITCH SIZE
110 X 71 yards

AWAY

CLOCK
(SOUTH STAND)

NORTH BANK STAND

GILLESPIE ROAD

LOWER

UPPER

DISABLED FANS

LOWER
EAST STAND
UPPER

AVENELL ROAD

# ASTON VILLA

## Villa Park, Trinity Road, Birmingham, B6 6HE

**Tel No:** 0121 327 2299
**Advance Tickets Tel No:** 0121 327 5353
**Fax:** 0121 322 2107
**Web Site:** www.avfc.co.uk
**E-Mail:** commercial.dept@astonvilla-fc.co.uk
**League:** F.A. Premier
**Brief History:** Founded in 1874. Founder Members Football League (1888). Former Grounds: Aston Park and Lower Aston Grounds and Perry Barr, moved to Villa Park (a development of the Lower Aston Grounds) in 1897. Record attendance 76,588
**(Total) Current Capacity:** 42,602 (all seated) (Prior to redevelopment)
**Visiting Supporters' Allocation:** Approx 2,983 in North Stand
**Club Colours:** Claret with blue stripe shirts, white shorts

**Nearest Railway Station:** Witton
**Parking (Car):** Asda car park, Aston Hall Road
**Parking (Coach/Bus):** Asda car park, Aston Hall Road (special coach park for visiting supporters situated in Witton Lane)
**Police Force and Tel No:** West Midlands (0121 322 6010)
**Disabled Visitors' Facilities:**
  **Wheelchairs:** Trinity Road Stand section
  **Blind:** Commentary by arrangement
**Anticipated Development(s):** In order to increase the ground's capacity to 51,000 Planning Permission has been obtained to extend the North Stand with two corner in-fills. There is, however, no confirmed timescale for the work to be completed.

### KEY
- **C** Club Offices
- **S** Club Shop
- **E** Entrance(s) for visiting supporters
- **R** Refreshment bars for visiting supporters
- **T** Toilets for visiting supporters

↑ North direction (approx)

- ❶ B4137 Witton Lane
- ❷ B4140 Witton Road
- ❸ Trinity Road
- ❹ A4040 Aston Lane to A34 Walsall Road
- ❺ To Aston Expressway & M6
- ❻ Holte End
- ❼ Visitors' Car Park
- ❽ To Witton railway station (100yd)
- ❾ North Stand
- ❿ Trinity Road Stand

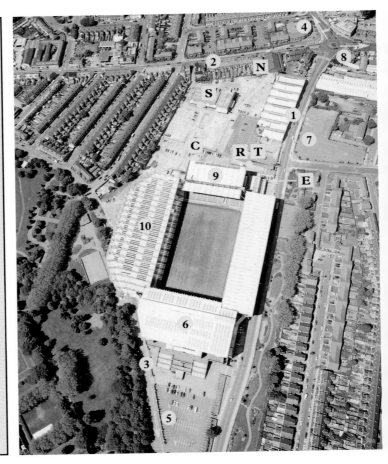

*Above: 688331; Right: 688329*

A season of frustration for the Villa faithful saw the team lose out to Birmingham City in the battle for supremacy in the West Midlands — West Brom were always going to be also rans — compounded by the team's inability to raise themselves above the lower levels of the Premiership. Indeed it was not until Villa defeated an already relegated Sunderland that Premiership survival was assured. Such was the nature of the team's performances during the course of the season that Graham Taylor felt it necessary to make an apology over the PA towards the end of the campaign. Without a dramatic upturn in fortunes in 2003/04 it looks as though it could be another hard year for Villa supporters. With the season over, Taylor decided that he'd had enough of the position and resigned. David O'Leary, the new incumbant will, however, face the same problems that Taylor had to deal with.

UPPER

MIDDLE

TRINITY ROAD STAND

LOWER

ROAD PASSES UNDERNEATH STAND

PITCH SIZE
105 X 69 metres

DISABLED ENCLOSURE

LOWER

UPPER

AWAY

NORTH STAND

WITTON ROAD

UPPER

HOLTE END STAND

LOWER

LOWER TIER

DOUG ELLIS STAND
(WITTON LANE STAND) UPPER TIER

WITTON LANE

HOLTE END

# BARNSLEY

## Oakwell Stadium, Grove Street, Barnsley, S71 1ET

**Tel No:** 01226 211211
**Advance Tickets Tel No:** 01226 211211
**Fax:** 01226 211444
**Web Site:** www.barnsleyfc.co.uk
**E-mail:** thereds@barnsleyfc.co.uk
**League:** 2nd Division
**Brief History:** Founded in 1887 as Barnsley St Peter's, changed name to Barnsley in 1897. Former Ground: Doncaster Road, Worsboro Bridge until 1888. Record attendance 40,255
**(Total) Current Capacity:** 23,200 (all seated)
**Visiting Supporters' Allocation:** 6,000 maximum (all seated; North Stand)
**Club Colours:** Red shirts, white shorts
**Nearest Railway Station:** Barnsley Exchange

**Parking (Car):** Queen's Ground car park
**Parking (Coach/Bus):** Queen's Ground car park
**Police Force and Tel No:** South Yorkshire (01266 206161)
**Disabled Visitors' Facilities:**
  **Wheelchairs:** Purpose Built Disabled Stand
  **Blind:** Commentary available
**Future Development(s):** With the completion of the new North Stand with its 6,000 capacity, the next phase for the redevelopment of Oakwell will feature the old West Stand with its remaining open seating. There is, however, no timescale for this work.

---

### KEY
**C** Club Offices
**S** Club Shop
**E** Entrance(s) for visiting supporters

↑ North direction (approx)

❶ A628 Pontefract Road
❷ To Barnsley Exchange BR station and M1 Junction 37 (two miles)
❸ Queen's Ground Car Park
❹ North Stand
❺ Grove Street
❻ To Town Centre

*Above:* 685529; *Right:* 685527

One of a number of teams to face an uncertain future — administration followed by a take-over by Peter Doyle which proved anything but straightforward — the club dispensed with the services of Steve Parkin in mid-October. Glyn Hodges took over on a caretaker basis with the administrators deciding not to make a permanent appointment until the club was out of administration. For much of the season, the team hovered around the relegation places, although, given the distractions of events off the field, finishing four points clear of the drop zone could be considered a success. However, with the Second Division in 2003/04 being potentially much stronger, the team could well struggle to survive at this level for another year. At least there is the potential for renewed derbies against another fallen giant in Sheffield Wednesday. A take-over during the summer saw Hodges dismissed and replaced by ex-Stoke boss Gudjon Thordarson

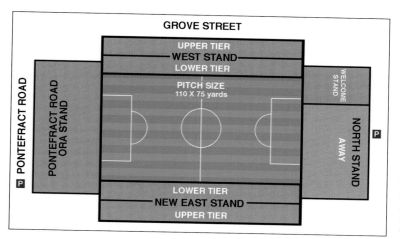

GROVE STREET

UPPER TIER
WEST STAND
LOWER TIER

PITCH SIZE
110 X 75 yards

LOWER TIER
NEW EAST STAND
UPPER TIER

PONTEFRACT ROAD

PONTEFRACT ROAD
ORA STAND

WELCOME STAND

NORTH STAND
AWAY

P

P

BARNSLEY FOOTBALL CLUB

# BIRMINGHAM CITY

## St Andrew's Stadium, St Andrew's Street, Birmingham, B9 4NH

**Tel No:** 0121 772 0101
**Advance Tickets Tel No:** 0121 772 0101
**Fax:** 0121 766 7866
**Web Site:** www.bcfc.com
**E-Mail:** reception@bcfc.com
**League:** FA Premiership
**Brief History:** Founded 1875, as Small Heath Alliance. Changed to Small Heath in 1888, Birmingham in 1905, Birmingham City in 1945. Former Grounds: Arthur Street, Ladypool Road, Muntz Street, moved to St Andrew's in 1906. Record attendance 68,844
**(Total) Current Capacity:** 30,016 (all seated)
**Visiting Supporters' Allocation:** 1-4,500 in new Railway End (Lower Tier)
**Club Colours:** Blue shirts, white shorts
**Nearest Railway Station:** Birmingham New Street

**Parking (Car):** Street parking
**Parking (Coach/Bus):** Coventry Road
**Police Force and Tel No:** West Midlands (0121 772 1169)
**Disabled Visitors' Facilities:**
**Wheelchairs:** 90 places; advanced notice required
**Blind:** Commentary available
**Future Development(s):** Following completion of the Railway End Stand, the final phase of the ground's redevelopment will feature the reconstruction of the old Main Stand. There are proposals for a new stand to take St Andrews' capacity to 36,500. Initially it was believed that this work would be undertaken if the Blues survived in the Premiership, but it has now been suggested that, if the club has money available, it will be used to strengthen the squad.

### KEY

**C** Club Offices
**S** Club Shop
**E** Entrance(s) for visiting supporters

↑ North direction (approx)

❶ Car Park
❷ B4128 Cattell Road
❸ Tilton Road
❹ Garrison Lane
❺ To A4540 & A38 (M)
❻ To City Centre and New Street BR Station (1½ miles)
❼ Railway End
❽ Tilton Road End
❾ Main Stand
❿ Kop Stand
⬤ Emmeline Street
⓬ Kingston Road
⓭ St Andrew's Street

*Above:* 679483; *Right:* 679479

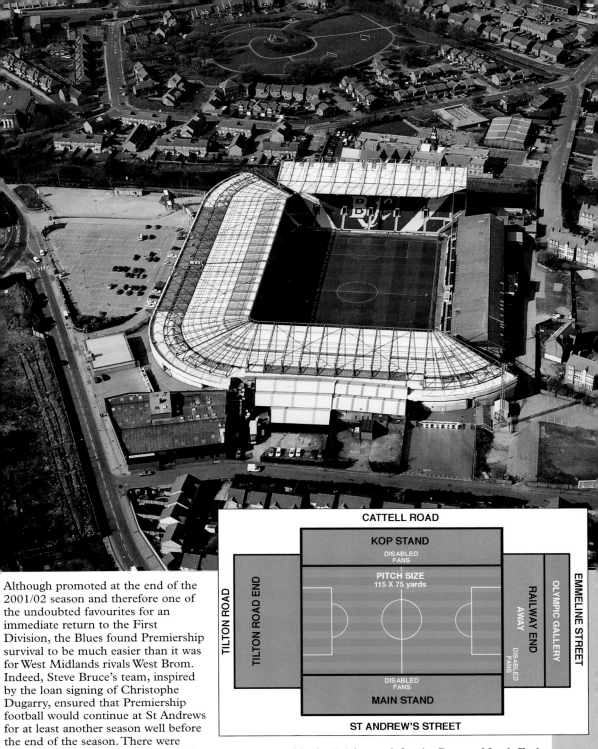

CATTELL ROAD

KOP STAND

DISABLED FANS

PITCH SIZE
115 X 75 yards

TILTON ROAD

TILTON ROAD END

RAILWAY END
AWAY

OLYMPIC GALLERY

EMMELINE STREET

DISABLED FANS

DISABLED FANS

MAIN STAND

ST ANDREW'S STREET

Although promoted at the end of the 2001/02 season and therefore one of the undoubted favourites for an immediate return to the First Division, the Blues found Premiership survival to be much easier than it was for West Midlands rivals West Brom. Indeed, Steve Bruce's team, inspired by the loan signing of Christophe Dugarry, ensured that Premiership football would continue at St Andrews for at least another season well before the end of the season. There were occasional blemishes in the season, however, most notably the 2-0 home defeat by Preston North End in the Worthington Cup. Overall, Blues' fans had the satisfaction of defeating Aston Villa to bring local supremacy (and watching their opponents concede one of the strangest own goals). However, as teams like Bradford and Ipswich have discovered, it's sometimes the second season in the Premiership that can prove more problematic and the key to City's survival in 2003/04 may well be how successful Bruce is in the transfer market during the summer.

# BLACKBURN ROVERS

## Ewood Park, Blackburn, Lancashire, BB2 4JF

**Tel No:** 01254 698888
**Advance Tickets Tel No:** 01254 671666
**Fax:** 01254 671042
**Web Site:** www.rovers.co.uk
**E-Mail:** commercial@rovers.co.uk
**League:** FA Premier
**Brief History:** Founded 1875. Former Grounds: Oozebooth, Pleasington Cricket Ground, Alexandra Meadows. Moved to Ewood Park in 1890. Founder members of Football League (1888). Record attendance 61,783
**(Total) Current Capacity:** 31,169 (all seated)
**Visiting Supporters' Allocation:** 3,914 at the Darwen End

**Club Colours:** Blue and white halved shirts, white shorts
**Nearest Railway Station:** Blackburn
**Parking (Car):** Street parking and c800 spaces at ground
**Parking (Coach/Bus):** As directed by Police
**Police Force and Tel No:** Lancashire (01254 51212)
**Disabled Visitors' Facilities:**
  **Wheelchairs:** All sides of the ground
  **Blind:** Commentary available
**Anticipated Development(s):** There is talk that the Riverside Stand may be rebuilt, but this is very tentative at this stage.

### KEY

**C** Club Offices
**S** Club Shop
**E** Entrance(s) for visiting supporters
**R** Refreshment bars for visiting supporters
**T** Toilets for visiting supporters

↑ North direction (approx)

❶ A666 Bolton Road
❷ Kidder Street
❸ Nuttall Street
❹ Town Centre & Blackburn Central BR station (1½ miles)
❺ To Darwen and Bolton
❻ Darwen End
❼ Car Parks
❽ Top O'Croft Road

*Above:* 692620; *Right:* 692614

successful season for Rovers saw Souness's team avoid 'second season syndrome' and thus
consolidate further its position in the Premiership. Having won the Worthington Cup during the
001/02 campaign, the season also witnessed Rovers' return to European action in the UEFA Cup. The
am's UEFA journey, however, ended in defeat by Celtic although the performance was impressive
cking only the essential away goal. In the Premiership, Blackburn finished in sixth place, thus assuring
e team another appearance in the UEFA Cup. Whilst it's now unlikely that Rovers will ever be able to
allenge for the highest honours in the Premiership — indeed few will be able to compete with the
uscle of Manchester United — Souness's success has certainly been to cement Rovers in the
emiership and this should again be achieved in 2003/04.

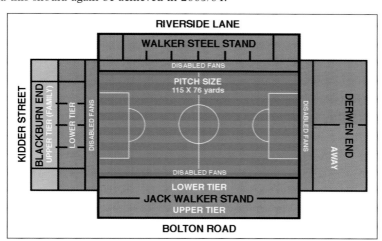

# BLACKPOOL

## Bloomfield Road, Blackpool, Lancashire, FY1 6JJ

**Tel No:** 0870 443 1953
**Advance Tickets Tel No:** 0870 443 1953
**Fax:** 01253 405011
**E-Mail:** info@blackpoolfc.co.uk
**Web Site:** www.blackpoolfc.co.uk
**League:** 2nd Division
**Brief History:** Founded 1887, merged with 'South Shore' (1899). Former grounds: Raikes Hall (twice) and Athletic Grounds, Stanley Park, South Shore played at Cow Cap Lane, moved to Bloomfield Road in 1899. Record attendance 38,098
**(Total) Current Capacity:** 11,000 (7,500 seated)
**Visiting Supporters' Allocation:** 2,700 (1,500 seated) in South Stand
**Club Colours:** Tangerine shirts, white shorts
**Nearest Railway Station:** Blackpool South

**Parking (Car):** At Ground and street parking (also behind West Stand – from M55)
**Parking (Coach/Bus):** Mecca car park (behind North End (also behind West Stand – from M55)
**Police Force and Tel No:** Lancashire (01253 293933)
**Disabled Visitors' Facilities:**
  **Wheelchairs:** North and West stands
  **Blind:** Commentary available (limited numbers)
**Anticipated Development(s):** The new West and North stands were completed for Christmas 2001 and future plans include the demolition of the South (Paddock) Stand and its replacement, to be followed by the reconstruction of the East Terrace. Once this work is completed, the capacity at Bloomfield Road will rise to 16,000 although there is currently no timescale as to when this work will take place.

---

### KEY

**C** Club Offices
**S** Club Shop
**E** Entrance(s) for visiting supporters

⬆ North direction (approx)

❶ Car Park
❷ To Blackpool South BR Station (1½ miles) and M55 Junction 4
❸ Bloomfield Drive
❹ Central Drive
❺ Henry Street
❻ East Paddock
❼ South Stand (away)
❽ West Stand
❾ North Stand

*Above:* 695529; *Right:* 695527

owing the success of finally achieving silverware in 2001/02 — OK it was the LDV Trophy but at
it brought some success to Bloomfield Road for the first time in nearly 50 years — much was
cted of Steve McMahon's team in 2002/03 with the Play-Offs certainly being within reach. In the
t, however, the team failed to live up to expectations and a mid-table finish — in 14th position more
20 points below the Play-Offs — was a disappointment. McMahon, however, retains his position
will no doubt be under pressure to see his team perform more strongly in the new season.

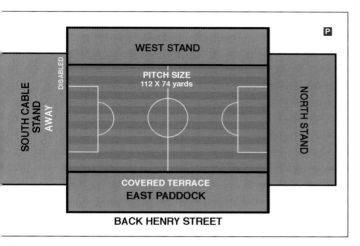

WEST STAND

PITCH SIZE
112 X 74 yards

DISABLED

SOUTH CABLE
STAND
AWAY

NORTH STAND

COVERED TERRACE
EAST PADDOCK

BACK HENRY STREET

# BOLTON WANDERERS

## Reebok Stadium, Burnden Way, Lostock, Bolton, BL6 6JW

**Tel No:** 01204 673673
**Advance Tickets Tel No:** 0871 871 2932
**Fax:** 01204 673773
**E-Mail:** reception@bwfc.co.uk
**Web Site:** www.bwfc.co.uk
**League:** FA Premiership
**Brief History:** Founded 1874 as Christ Church; name changed 1877. Former grounds: Several Fields, Pikes Lane (1880-95) and Burnden Park (1895-1997). Moved to Reebok Stadium for 1997/98 season. Record attendance (Burnden Park): 69,912. Record attendance of 27,351 at Reebok Stadium
**(Total) Current Capacity:** 27,879 (all-seater)
**Visiting Supporters' Allocation:** 5,200 (South Stand)
**Club Colours:** White shirts, blue shorts

**Nearest Railway Station:** Horwich Parkway
**Parking (Car):** 2,800 places at ground with up 3,000 others in proximity
**Parking (Coach/Bus):** As directed
**Police Force and Tel No:** Greater Manchester (01204 522466)
**Disabled Visitors' Facilities:**
**Wheelchairs:** c100 places around the ground
**Blind:** Commentary available
**Anticipated Developments(s):** The station at Horwich Parkway has now opened. There are currently no further plans for the development of the Reebok Stadium.

---

### KEY

↑ North direction (approx)

❶ Junction 6 of M61
❷ A6027 Horwich link road
❸ South Stand (away)
❹ North Stand
❺ Nat Lofthouse Stand
❻ West Stand
❼ M61 northbound to M6 and Preston (at J6)
❽ M61 southbound to Manchester (at J6)
❾ To Horwich and Bolton
❿ To Lostock Junction BR station
● Horwich Parkway station

20

*Above: 688307; Right: 688303*

Threatened by relegation for much of the season, Sam Allardyce's team again achieved the great escape with victory over Middlesbrough on the final day consigning West Ham United to the First Division. As in the previous season, Wanderers achieved some highly impressive results, but continued to find a winning run impossible. Thus fans faced another 'edge of the seat' season with the team hovering about the drop zone. One facility that Allardyce seems to have is the ability to bring in talented players who seem capable of turning the season round — in 2002/03 it was Jay-Jay Okacha — and so long as he is able to do so, then Bolton's position, whilst never strong, will be better. In 2003/04 Bolton ought to be able to maintain its Premiership position with greater ease than before: the promoted teams don't look as strong (with the possible exception of Wolves) and a couple of existing Premiership teams (possibly Fulham or Leeds) may struggle.

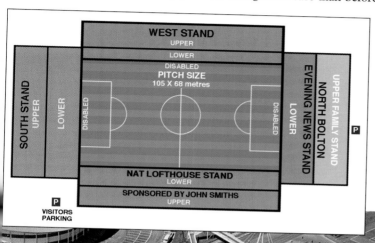

# BOSTON UNITED

## York Street, Boston, Lincolnshire PE21 6JN

**Club Offices:** 14-16 Spain Place, Boston, Lincolnshire PE21 6HN
**Tel No:** 01205 364406
**Advance Tickets Tel No:** 01205 364406
**Fax:** 01205 354063
**Web Site:** www.bostonunited.co.uk
**E-mail:** jan.mclucas@playing4success.org.uk
**League:** 3rd Division
**Brief History:** Boston Town was established in the 1880s and commenced playing at York Street. The club dropped the 'Town' suffix after World War 1 and re-formed as Boston United in 1934. The team won the Conference title in 1977 but was not allowed into the league due to the standard of the ground. The title was won again in 2002 and the club entered the Nationwide League at the start of the 2002/03 season. Record attendance 11,000
**(Total) Current Capacity:** 6,643 (1,769 seated)

**Visiting Supporters' Allocation:** 1,800 (no seated) in Town End Terrace
**Club Colours:** Amber and black striped shirts, black shorts
**Nearest Railway Station:** Boston (one mile)
**Parking (Car):** Limited parking at the ground; recommended car park is the John Adams NCP
**Parking (Coach/Bus):** As directed
**Police Force and Tel No:** Lincolnshire (01205 366222)
**Disabled Visitors Facilities:**
  **Wheelchairs:** Finn Forest Stand
  **Blind:** No special facility
**Future Development(s):** The club intends to relocate and is seeking to move to a new site to the east of the town for which planning permission is being sought. There is, as yet, no confirmed timescale for the work.

### KEY

**E** Entrance(s) for visiting supporters
**R** Refreshment bars for visiting supporters
**T** Toilets for visiting supporters

↑ North direction (approx)

❶ John Adams Way
❷ Spilsby Road
❸ Haven Bridge Road
❹ York Street
❺ Spayne Road
❻ River Witham
❼ Maud Foster Drain
❽ Market Place
❾ To bus and railway stations
❿ York Street Stand (away)
⓫ Spayne Road Terrace
⓬ Town End Terrace
⓭ Finnforest Stand

*Above:* 693105; *Right:* 693098

uring the close season in 2002 it was by no means certain that Boston's promotion to the Football
eague would be confirmed. However, the club was allowed to retain its Third Division status although
enalised by four points and with manager Steve Evans and chairman departing. New manager Neil
hompson was faced by the handicap of the deducted points and, unlike many recently promoted
onference teams, the Pilgrims struggled at the higher level. In the event, however, despite hovering
st above the drop zone for much of the campaigns a late improvement in form saw the team move
to a position of mid-table
curity. The relative success of
002/03, where consolidation
as probably the order of the
iy, means that the team has
ilt a good platform for
rther development in
003/04.

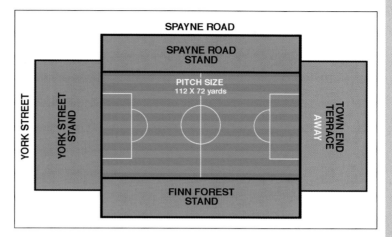

# A.F.C. BOURNEMOUTH

## The Fitness First Stadium at Dean Court, Bournemouth, Dorset, BH7 7AF

**Tel No:** 01202 726300
**Advance Tickets Tel No:** 0845 011 2322
**Fax:** 01202 726301
**E-Mail:** enquiries@afcb.co.uk
**Web Site:** www.afcb.co.uk
**League:** 2nd Division
**Brief History:** Founded 1890 as Boscombe St. John's, changed to Boscombe (1899), Bournemouth & Boscombe Athletic (1923) and A.F.C. Bournemouth (1971). Former grounds Kings Park (twice) and Castlemain Road, Pokesdown. Moved to Dean Court in 1910. Record attendance 28,799
**(Total) Current Capacity:** 9,600 (all seated)
**Visiting Supporters' Allocation:** 1,160 in East Stand (can be increased to 2,000 if required)
**Club Colours:** Red and black shirts, black shorts
**Nearest Railway Station:** Bournemouth

**Parking (Car):** Large car park adjacent ground
**Parking (Coach/Bus):** Large car park adjacent ground
**Police Force and Tel No:** Dorset (01202 552099)
**Disabled Visitors' Facilities:**
  **Wheelchairs:** 100 spaces
  **Blind:** No special facility
**Anticipated Development(s):** Following the completion of the first three stands at the new Dean Court, attention has turned to the possibility of constructing the fourth stand. Once completed, this will take Dean Court's capacity to 12,000 all-seated (although there is some debate as to whether this new facility will be terraced). There is, however, no current time-scale for the work.

### KEY

**C** Club Offices

↑ North direction (approx)

❶ Car Park
❷ A338 Wessex Way
❸ To Bournemouth BR Station (1½ miles)
❹ To A31 & M27
❺ Thistlebarrow Road
❻ King's Park Drive
❼ Littledown Avenue
❽ North Stand
❾ Main Stand
❿ East Stand

*Above:* 695760; *Right:* 695749

ollowing relegation at the end of 2001/02, the Cherries faced the new campaign in the Third Division. nder Sean O'Driscoll, the team was never quite good enough to maintain a strong challenge for utomatic promotion, finishing fourth, some 10 points off promoted Wrexham with a much inferior al difference. However, this brought the team in to the Play-offs, where it faced Bury in the semi- als. Victory over the two legs meant that the Cherries faced Lincoln City in the final at the Millennium Stadium. A triumphant day in Cardiff saw Bournemouth not only become the first team in history to score five goals in a Play-Off final but also overpower Lincoln to regain the team's Second Division status after an absence of just a year. However, as with all teams promoted, and particularly those who achieve success through the Play-Offs, the first season at the higher level may prove difficult.

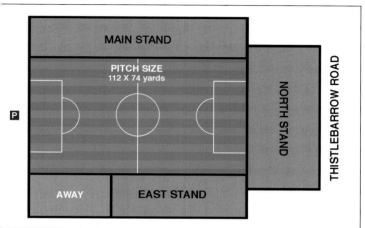

MAIN STAND

PITCH SIZE
112 X 74 yards

NORTH STAND

THISTLEBARROW ROAD

P

AWAY

EAST STAND

# BRADFORD CITY

## Bradford & Bingley Stadium, Valley Parade, Bradford, BD8 7DY

**Tel No:** 01274 773355
**Advance Tickets Tel No:** 01274 770022
**Fax:** 01274 773356
**Web Site:** www.bradfordcityfc.co.uk
**E-Mail:** bradfordcityfc@compuserve.com
**League:** 1st Division
**Brief History:** Founded 1903 (formerly Manningham Northern Union Rugby Club founded in 1876). Continued use of Valley Parade, joined 2nd Division on re-formation. Record attendance: 39,146
**(Total) Current Capacity:** 25,136 (all seated)
**Visiting Supporters' Allocation:** 1,842 (all seated) in Symphony stand
**Club Colours:** Claret and amber shirts, black shorts
**Nearest Railway Station:** Bradford Forster Square
**Parking (Car):** Street parking and car parks

**Parking (Coach/Bus):** As directed by Police
**Police Force and Tel No:** West Yorkshire (01274 723422)
**Disabled Visitors' Facilities:**
  **Wheelchairs:** 110 places in Sunwin, CIBA and Carlsberg stands
  **Blind:** Commentary available
**Anticipated Development(s):** With work on the Main (Sunwin) Stand now completed, Valley Parade has a slightly imbalanced look. The club has proposals for the reconstruction of the Midland Road (CIBA) Stand to take the ground's capacity to 30,000, although, given the club's current financial position, there is no time-scale.

| KEY | |
|---|---|
| **C** | Club Offices |
| **S** | Club Shop |
| **E** | Entrance(s) for visiting supporters |
| **R** | Refreshment bars for visiting supporters |
| **T** | Toilets for visiting supporters |

⬆ North direction (approx)

❶ Midland Road
❷ Valley Parade
❸ A650 Manningham Lane
❹ To City Centre, Forster Square and Interchange BR Stations M606 & M62
❺ To Keighley
❻ Car Parks
❼ Sunwin Stand
❽ Midland (CIBA) Stand
❾ Symphony Stand
❿ Carlsberg Stand

*Above: 692550; Right: 692545*

**MIDLAND ROAD**

UPPER
LOWER

**CIBA STAND**

| A | B | C | D | E | F | G |

DISABLED FANS

**AWAY**

**PITCH SIZE**
113 X 75

DISABLED FANS

**THORNCLIFFE ROAD**

**CARLSBERG STAND**

| M | L | K | J | H | G |
| F | E | D | C | B | A |

| F | E | D | C | B | A |
| N | M | L | K | J | H | G |

**HOLYWELL ASH LANE**

**SYMPHONY STAND**

| LA | UF |
| LB | UG |
| LC | UH |
| LD | UJ |
| LE | UK |

LOWER
UPPER

**SOUTH PARADE**

t the start of the 2002/03 campaign, City fans were mply grateful to have a am to support, given the am's administration uring the close season and he very real threat that the uthorities would bar the am from the League. In the event, the new campaign started reasonably well for Nicky Law's team but as the campaign wore n the combination of injuries and the restrictions placed on the team in terms of recruitment took eir toll and the team were sucked into events at the wrong end of the table. Survival in the First ivision was assured, however, and with the team out of administration under a new chairman the antams will again feature in the First Division. With the playing squad much reduced and with udgets still tight, City will undoubtedly be seen as one of the potential favourites for relegation. One f the high points of the 2002/03 campaign was undoubtedly the emergence — by necessity — of veral talented young players and this promise could yet ensure First Division survival.

# BRENTFORD

## Griffin Park, Braemar Road, Brentford, Middlesex, TW8 0NT

**Tel No:** 020 8847 2511
**Advance Tickets Tel No:** 020 8847 2511
**Fax:** 020 8568 9940
**Web Site:** www.brentfordfc.co.uk
**E-Mail:** enquiries@brentfordfc.co.uk
**League:** 2nd Division
**Brief History:** Founded 1889. Former Grounds: Clifden House Ground, Benn's Field (Little Ealing), Shotters Field, Cross Roads, Boston Park Cricket Ground, moved to Griffin Park in 1904. Founder-members Third Division (1920). Record attendance 38,678
**(Total) Current Capacity:** 12,416 (8,905 seated)
**Visiting Supporters' Allocation:** 2,200 on Ealing Road Terrace (open) and 600 seats in Block A of Braemar Road Stand
**Club Colours:** Red and white striped shirts, black shorts
**Nearest Railway Station:** Brentford, South Ealing (tube)

**Parking (Car):** Street parking (restricted)
**Parking (Coach/Bus):** Layton Road car park
**Police Force and Tel No:** Metropolitan (020 8577 1212)
**Disabled Visitors' Facilities:**
**Wheelchairs:** Braemar Road
**Blind:** Commentary available
**Anticipated Development(s):** After some years of debate, where relocation to Feltham seemed likely, the club announced in November 2002 that it was planning to relocate to a site near Kew, about a mile from Griffin Park. It is expected that Griffin Park will be sold and that the club will seek planning permission to construct a new 25,000-seat ground at the new site. There is, however, no confirmed timescale for the work. It is also likely that the new ground will be shared with the London Broncos RLFC, who are currently playing their home games at Griffin Park.

### KEY

**C** Club Offices
**S** Club Shop

↑ North direction (approx)

❶ Ealing Road
❷ Braemar Road
❸ Brook Road South
❹ To M4 (1/4 mile) & South Ealing Tube Station(1 mile)
❺ Brentford BR Station
❻ To A315 High Street & Kew Bridge
❼ New Road
❽ Ealing Road Terrace (away)
❾ Brook Road Stand

*Above:* 695938; *Right:* 695940

NEW ROAD

NEW STAND

PITCH SIZE
110 X 73 yards

BROOK ROAD STAND

COVERED TERRACE

SEATS

DISABLED
FANS

EALING ROAD
TERRACE
UNCOVERED TERRACE

AWAY

EALING ROAD

PADDOCK

BRAEMAR ROAD STAND

AWAY

BRAEMAR ROAD

After the disappointment of the team's failure to achieve promotion through the Play-Offs at the end of the 2001/02 season with the consequent departure of manager Steve Coppell and the loss of several influential players, tyro manager Wally Downes did well initially to keep the team up with the early season pace-makers. However, loss of form from d-season onwards resulted in the team gradually drifting down the Second Division table with, at one ge, the serious threat that the team would get dragged into the relegation battle. In the event, the Bees ished in 16th spot and, with the young team now much more experienced, confidence at Griffin Park 2003/04 should be high.

# BRIGHTON & HOVE ALBION

## Withdean Stadium, Tongdean Lane, Brighton BN1 5JD

**Tel No:** 01273 778855
**Fax:** 01273 321095
**Advance Ticket Tel No:** 01273 776992
**Web Site:** www.seagulls.co.uk
**E-Mail:** seagulls@bhafc.co.uk
**League:** 2nd Division
**Brief History:** Founded 1900 as Brighton & Hove Rangers, changed to Brighton & Hove Albion 1902. Former grounds: Home Farm (Withdean), County Ground, Goldstone Ground (1902-1997), Priestfield Stadium (ground share with Gillingham) 1997-1999; moved to Withdean Stadium 1999. Founder members of the 3rd Division 1920. Record attendance (at Goldstone Ground): 36,747; at Withdean Stadium: 6,995.
**(Total) Current Capacity:** c7,000 (all seated)
**Visiting Supporters' Allocation:** 325 (North Stand) (min)
**Club Colours:** Blue and white striped shirts, white shorts
**Nearest Railway Station:** Preston Park
**Parking (Cars):** Street parking in the immediate vicinity of the ground is residents' only. This will be strictly enforced and it is suggested that intending visitors should use parking facilities away from the ground and use the proposed park and ride bus services that will be provided.
**Parking (Coach/Bus):** As directed
**Police Force and Tel No:** Sussex (01273 778922)
**Disabled Visitors' Facilities**
  **Wheelchairs:** Facilities in both North and South stands
  **Blind:** No special facility
**Anticipated Development(s):** Towards the end of 2002 the club announced that it was now planning to construct the 25,000-seat ground at Falmer as one development — previously it had contemplated constructing a ground with a 12,500-seat capacity as a first stage — and that the plans would be the subject of a public enquiry in early 2003. Given the lack of progress thus far, expect the Seagulls to be based at Withdean for at least another season. The club is interested in increasing the capacity at Withdean Stadium, but these proposals are meeting local resistance.

---

### KEY
**Club Address:**
  44 North Road, Brighton
  BN1 1YR
  Tel: 01273 695460
  Fax: 01273 648179

**Shop Address:**
  6 Queen's Road, Brighton

⬆ North direction (approx)

Note: All games at Withdean will be all-ticket with no cash admissions on the day.

❶ Withdean Stadium
❷ London-Brighton railway line
❸ London Road (A23)
❹ Tongdean Lane
❺ Valley Drive
❻ To Brighton town centre and main railway station (1.75 miles)
❼ Tongdean Lane (with bridge under railway)
❽ South Stand
❾ A23 northwards to Crawley
❿ To Preston Park railway station
● North Stand

*Above:* 695745; *Right:* 695788

ving had two successive promotions, the Seagulls were always going to face the new season in vision One with difficulty and so it proved. After 10 successive defeats, Martin Hinshelwood was ved upstairs and experienced manager Steve Coppell was brought in to the Withdean hotseat in ly October. Although the club did start to pick up some points, the early season form — when the m lost a dozen games on the trot — meant that it was always going to be struggle to survive. All credit to the team, therefore, that under Coppell's astute management the team's fate was not determined until the last Sunday of the season. Unfortunately a draw at already relegated Grimsby combined with Stoke's 1-0 win over Reading consigned the Seagulls to the second Division. Whether the team makes an immediate challenge for promotion, as Crewe did in 2002/03, will depend to a significant extent on retaining Bobby Zamora and on the experienced Coppell remaining.

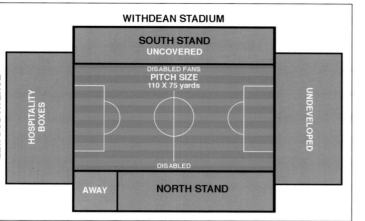

**WITHDEAN STADIUM**

SOUTH STAND
UNCOVERED

DISABLED FANS
PITCH SIZE
110 X 75 yards

HOSPITALITY BOXES

UNDEVELOPED

DISABLED

AWAY

NORTH STAND

# BRISTOL CITY

## Ashton Gate Stadium, Ashton Road, Bristol BS3 2EJ

**Tel No:** 0117 963 0630
**Advance Tickets Tel No:** 0117 966 6666
**Fax:** 0117 963 0700
**Web Site:** www.bcfc.co.uk
**E-Mail:** commercial@bcfc.co.uk
**League:** 2nd Division
**Brief History:** Founded 1894 as Bristol South End changed to Bristol City in 1897. Former Ground: St John's Lane, Bedminster, moved to Ashton Gate in 1904. Record attendance 43,335
**(Total) Current Capacity:** 21,497 (all seated)
**Visiting Supporters' Allocation:** 3,000 in Wedlock End (all seated; can be increased to 5,500 if necessary)
**Club Colours:** Red shirts, white shorts
**Nearest Railway Station:** Bristol Temple Meads
**Parking (Car):** Street parking

**Parking (Coach/Bus):** Marsh Road
**Police Force and Tel No:** Avon/Somerset (0117 927 7777)
**Disabled Visitors' Facilities:**
  **Wheelchairs:** Limited
  **Blind:** Commentary available
**Anticipated Development(s):** At the end of November, Bristol city council announced that it was withdrawing from the scheme to construct a new stadium for the city and that any future development would be the responsibility of the club. The club has plans to redevelop three sides — the Williams, Wedlock and Dolman stands in that sequence — of Ashton Gate taking the ground's total capacity to 30,000. Planning permission for the work has been granted and work could commence during 2004.

### KEY

**C** Club Offices
**S** Club Shop
**E** Entrance(s) for visiting supporters

⬆ North direction (approx)

**❶** A370 Ashton Road
**❷** A3209 Winterstoke Road
**❸** To Temple Meads Station (1½ miles
**❹** To City Centre, A4, M32 & M4
**❺** Database Wedlock Stand
**❻** Atyeo Stand

*Above: 692242; Right: 692240*

aving just missed the Play-Offs at the end of 2001/02, under Danny Wilson the Robins continued to make ogress in 2002/03 as one of the teams chasing the second automatic promotion spot (Wigan were so far ead for the duration that their promotion seemed a foregone conclusion almost from day one). In the ent, the team finished third, three points behind Crewe and thus entered the Play-Offs, where the Robins faced Cardiff in the semi-finals. Unfortunately, City were unable to overturn a 1-0 score line from Ninian Park in the home leg and, therefore, Second Division football will again be on offer at Ashton Gate this season. City ought to be one of the pre-season favourites to make the Play-Offs at worst.

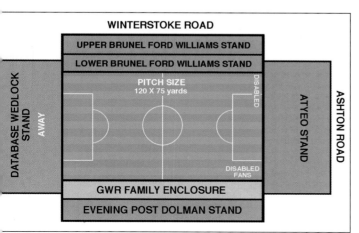

# BRISTOL ROVERS

## The Memorial Stadium, Filton Avenue, Horfield, Bristol BS7 0BF

**Tel No:** 0117 909 6648
**Advance Tickets Tel No:** 0117 924 7474
**Fax:** 0117 908 5530
**Web Site:** www.bristolrovers.co.uk
**E-Mail:** admin@bristolrovers.co.uk
**League:** 3rd Division
**Brief History:** Founded 1883 as Black Arabs, changed to Eastville Rovers (1884), Bristol Eastville Rovers (1896) and Bristol Rovers (1897). Former grounds: Purdown, Three Acres, The Downs (Horfield), Ridgeway, Bristol Stadium (Eastville), Twerton Park (1986-96), moved to The Memorial Ground 1996. Record attendance: (Eastville) 38,472, (Twerton Park) 9,813, (Memorial Ground) 9,274
**(Total) Current Capacity:** 11,917 (4,000 seated); standing capacity of 8,000 includes 500 on the Family Terrace
**Visiting Supporters' Allocation:** 1,132 (Centenary Stand Terrace)

**Club Colours:** Blue and white quartered shirts, white shorts
**Nearest Railway Station:** Filton or Stapleton Road
**Parking (Car):** Limited parking at ground for home fans only; street parking also available
**Parking (Coach/Bus):** As directed
**Police Force and Tel No:** Avon/Somerset (0117 927 7777)
**Disabled Visitors' Facilities:**
**Wheelchairs:** 35 wheelchair positions
**Blind:** Limited provision
**Anticipated Development(s):** The club has ambitious plans for the development of the Memorial Ground. This work will probably include the replacement of the Centenary Stand and Terrace as well as the South Stand. The club is aiming for a stadium with a 20,000-seat capacity subject to finance. There is, as yet, no confirmed timescale for the work.

### KEY

**C** Rugby Club offices
**E** Entrance(s) for visiting supporters
**R** Refrshments for visiting supporters
**T** Toilets for visiting supporters

⬆ North direction (approx)

❶ Filton Avenue
❷ Gloucester Road
❸ Muller Road
❹ To Bristol city centre (2.5 miles) and BR Temple Meads station (3 miles)
❺ Downer Road
❻ Car Park
❼ To M32 J2 (1.5 miles)
❽ Strathmore Road
❾ To Filton (1.5 miles)
❿ Centenary Stand
● West Stand

*Above: 692206; Right: 692197*

elegated at the end of 2001/02, the Gasheads were one of the pre-season favourites for challenging for
omotion back to the Second Division. Indeed, the team did make a serious challenge to depart from
e Third — unfortunately, however, it was at the wrong end of the table and, for much of the season,
legation to the Conference seemed a serious possibility. In the event, results towards the end of the
ason ensured that Ray Graydon's team survived to battle in the Third Division again in 2003/04.
owever, with two-up/two-down to the Conference and with two ambitious teams making the leap for
the start of the 2003/04 season, Rovers will need to see a dramatic improvement in form if League football is to be seen at the Memorial Stadium in 2004/05.

MULLER ROAD

CENTENARY STAND

AWAY

DISABLED
FANS

PITCH SIZE
110 X 74 yards

BLACKTHORN
END

SOUTH STAND

DISABLED
FANS

FAMILY TERRACE

WEST STAND

# BURNLEY

## Turf Moor, Harry Potts Way, Burnley, Lancs, BB10 4BX

**Tel No:** 0870 443 1882
**Advance Tickets Tel No:** 0870 443 1914
**Fax:** 01282 700014
**Web Site:** www.burnleyfootballclub.com
**E-Mail:** info@burnleyfootballclub.net
**League:** 2nd Division
**Brief History:** Founded 1882, Burnley Rovers (Rugby Club) combined with another Rugby Club, changed to soccer and name to Burnley. Moved from Calder Vale to Turf Moor in 1882. Founder-members Football League (1888). Record attendance 54,775
**(Total) Current Capacity:** 22,000 (all seated)
**Visiting Supporters' Allocation:** 4,125 (all seated in Lookers [Cricket Field] Stand)

**Club Colours:** Claret with blue sleeved shirts, white with claret and blue trim shorts
**Nearest Railway Station:** Burnley Central
**Parking (Car):** Church Street and Fulledge Rec. (car parks)
**Parking (Coach/Bus):** As directed by Police
**Police Force and Tel No:** Lancashire (01282 425001)
**Disabled Visitors' Facilities:**
　**Wheelchairs:** Places available in North, East and Cricket Field stands
　**Blind:** Headsets provided with commentary
**Anticipated Development(s):**

### KEY

**C** Club Offices
**S** Club Shop
**E** Entrance(s) for visiting supporters

⬆ North direction (approx)

❶ Brunshaw Road
❷ Belvedere Road
❸ Burnley Central BR Station (¹/₂ mile)
❹ Cricket Ground
❺ Cricket Field Stand
❻ East (Jimmy McIlroy) Stand
❼ Bob Lord Stand
❽ North (James Hargreaves) Stand

er a hugely successful 2001/02 season, when Stan Ternent's Clarets just failed to make the Play-Offs
he end of their first campaign back in the First Division, much was expected of the team in
02/03. Unfortunately, the team suffered a serious bout of second-seasonitis and struggled to make
ch of an impact. A position of mid-table security, in 16th place, was regarded by the manager as
ng wholly unsatisfactory and Ternent has promised that the squad will be revamped for the start of
2003/04. The team is now pretty well established back in the First Division and how far it prospers in the new campaign will depend significantly on how quickly any new faces are integrated into the rest of the team. One bright spot in an otherwise lacklustre season was a 2-1 victory over Spurs at Turf Moor in the Worthington Cup.

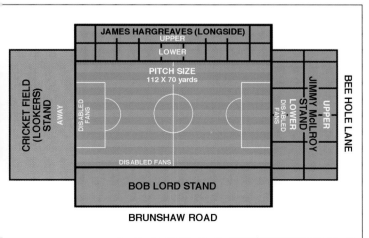

# BURY

## Gigg Lane, Bury, Lancashire, BL9 9HR

**Tel No:** 0161 764 4881
**Advance Tickets Tel No:** 0161 705 2144
**Fax:** 0161 764 5521
**Web Site:** www.buryfc.co.uk
**E-Mail:** info@buryfc.co.uk
**League:** 3rd Division
**Brief History:** Founded 1885, no former names or former grounds. Record attendance 35,000
**(Total) Current Capacity:** 11,669 (all seated)
**Visiting Supporters' Allocation:** 2,676 (all seated) in West Stand
**Club Colours:** White shirts, royal blue shorts
**Nearest Railway Station:** Bury Interchange

**Parking (Car):** Street parking
**Parking (Coach/Bus):** As directed by Police
**Police Force and Tel No:** Greater Manchester (0161 872 5050)
**Disabled Visitors' Facilities:**
  **Wheelchairs:** South Stand (home) and West Stand (away)
  **Blind:** Commentary available
**Anticipated Development(s):** The completion of the rebuilt Cemetery End means that current plans for the redevelopment of Gigg Lane have been completed.

---

*KEY*

**C** Club Offices
**S** Club Shop
**E** Entrance(s) for visiting supporters

⬆ North direction (approx)

❶ Car Park
❷ Gigg Lane
❸ A56 Manchester Road
❹ Town Centre & Bury Interchange (Metrolink) (³/₄ mile)
❺ West (Manchester Road) Stand
❻ Cemetery End

*Above: 684931; Right: 684926*

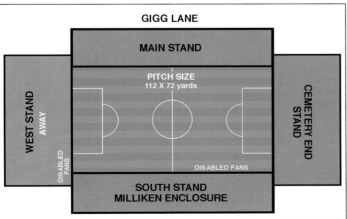

**GIGG LANE**

**MAIN STAND**

**PITCH SIZE**
112 X 72 yards

**WEST STAND**

**AWAY**

**DISABLED FANS**

**CEMETERY END STAND**

**DISABLED FANS**

**SOUTH STAND**
**MILLIKEN ENCLOSURE**

After the traumas of the 2001/02 season, when the Shakers faced both Administration and relegation to the Third Division, under Andy Preece 2002/03 was a season of some success on the field with the team managing to hold on to seventh place — and thus entry into the Play-Offs — despite a last-day defeat at Gigg Lane to already-promoted Wrexham. In the Play-Off semi-finals, the team faced Bournemouth. After a 0-0 draw at Gigg Lane, the Shakers were defeated 3-1 at Dean Court, thereby ensuring Third Division

otball in 2003/04. If the team can maintain its progress, then fans can expect another serious push wards promotion.

# CAMBRIDGE UNITED

## Abbey Stadium, Newmarket Road, Cambridge, CB5 8LN

**Tel No:** 01223 566500
**Advance Tickets Tel No:** 01223 566500
**Fax:** 01223 566502
**Web Site:** www.cambridge-united.co.uk
**E-mail:** web@cambridge-united.co.uk
**League:** 3rd Division
**Brief History:** Founded 1913 as Abbey United, changed to Cambridge United in 1951. Former Grounds: Midsummer Common, Stourbridge Common, Station Farm Barnwell (The Celery Trenches) & Parker's Piece, moved to Abbey Stadium in 1933. Record attendance 14,000
**(Total) Current Capacity:** 9,617 (4,784 seated)
**Visiting Supporters' Allocation:** c1,000 (covered terrace on south end of the Habbin Stand) or 1,600 seats on the new South Stand.
**Club Colours:** Amber and black shirts, amber shorts
**Nearest Railway Station:** Cambridge (2 miles)

**Parking (Car):** Coldhams Common
**Parking (Coach/Bus):** Coldhams Common
**Police Force and Tel No:** Cambridge (01223 358966)
**Disabled Visitors' Facilities:**
  **Wheelchairs:** Limited number that should be pre-booked
  **Blind:** No special facility
**Anticipated Development(s):** The new South Stand has now been completed. This is the first stage of a plan to turn the ground into a 10,000-capacity all-seater stadium. The new stand has been moved some 15m to the south, thereby allowing for a slight adjustment to the pitch. The next phase in the redevelopment will cover the North stand, which will be replaced with a 3,500-seat structure that will also include 14 executive boxes.

| KEY | |
| --- | --- |
| **E** | Entrance(s) for visiting supporters |
| **R** | Refreshment bars for visiting supporters |
| **T** | Toilets for visiting supporters |
| ↑ | North direction (approx) |
| ❶ | A1134 Newmarket Road |
| ❷ | To A11 for Newmarket |
| ❸ | To City Centre, Cambridge BR Station (2 miles) and M11 |
| ❹ | Whitehill Road |
| ❺ | South Stand |
| ❻ | Habbin Stand |
| ❼ | Main Stand |
| ❽ | North Terrace |

*Above: 695786; Right: 695782*

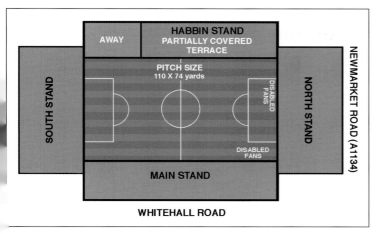

SOUTH STAND

AWAY

**HABBIN STAND**
**PARTIALLY COVERED**
**TERRACE**

**PITCH SIZE**
110 X 74 yards

DISABLED FANS

DISABLED FANS

NORTH STAND

**NEWMARKET ROAD (A1134)**

**MAIN STAND**

**WHITEHALL ROAD**

A season of mid-table mediocrity for John Taylor's side saw United finish the Third Division campaign in 12th position. Never involved in either the promotion or relegation battles, the 2002/03 season can perhaps be regarded by the Abbey Stadium faithful as one of consolidation.

# CARDIFF CITY

## Ninian Park, Sloper Road, Cardiff, CF11 8SX

**Tel No:** 029 2022 1001
**Advance Tickets Tel No:** 0845 345 1400
**Fax:** 029 2034 1148
**Web Site:** www.cardiffcityfc.co.uk
**E-mail:** admin@cardiffcityfc.co.uk
**League:** 1st Division
**Brief History:** Founded 1899. Former Grounds: Riverside Cricket Club, Roath, Sophia Gardens, Cardiff Arms Park and The Harlequins Rugby Ground, moved to Ninian Park in 1910. Ground record attendance 61,566 (Wales v. England, 1961)
**(Total) Current Capacity:** 22,000 (12,647 seated)
**Visiting Supporters' Allocation:** 2,000 maximum in Carling Grange End Terrace (no seated)
**Club Colours:** Blue shirts, blue shorts
**Nearest Railway Station:** Ninian Park (adjacent) (Cardiff Central 1 mile)

**Parking (Car):** Opposite Ground, no street parking around ground
**Parking (Coach/Bus):** Leckwith Stadium car park
**Police Force and Tel No:** South Wales (029 2022 2111)
**Disabled Visitors' Facilities:**
  **Wheelchairs:** Corner Canton Stand/Popular Bank (covered)
  **Blind:** No special facility
**Anticipated Development(s):** Although the long term aim of chairman Sam Hammam is to relocate to a new 60,000-seat stadium that will replace the existing Leckwith Stadium for the start of the 2004/05 season, limited work, including the addition of seats to the Popular Side and the roofing of the Grange End Terrace, was completed by the start of the 2001/02 season.

**KEY**

**C** Club Offices
**S** Club Shop
**E** Entrance(s) for visiting supporters
**R** Refreshment bars for visiting supporters
**T** Toilets for visiting supporters (Terrace only, when used)

↑ North direction (approx)

❶ Sloper Road
❷ B4267 Leckwith Road
❸ Car Park
❹ To A4232 & M4 Junction 33 (8 miles)
❺ Ninian Park Road
❻ To City Centre & Cardiff Central BR Station (1 mile)
❼ To A48 Western Avenue, A49M, and M4 Junction 32 and 29
❽ Ninian Park BR station

*Above: 693234; Right: 693243*

llowing the failure in the Play-Offs at the end of 2001/02 and with Chairman Sam Hammam eager
 further advancement, the Bluebirds were always going to be one of the pre-season favourites for
omotion and Lennie Lawrence's team did not disappoint, with the team vying for one of the
tomatic promotion spots right until the end of the season. In the event, however, Cardiff rather lost
ir way in the last few games, ultimately finishing in sixth place, one point above Tranmere Rovers

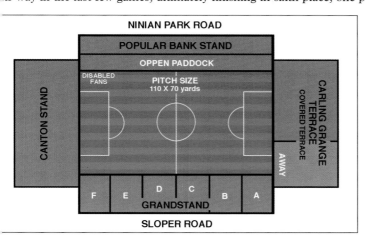

but with a much better goal difference. Having again achieved the Play-Offs, Cardiff faced Bristol City in the semi-finals. Victory ensured that there would be a 'home' team in the Play-Off final against QPR and, despite being outplayed for much of the normal 90min, City scored the only goal in extra time to bring First Division football the Ninian Park for the first time in almost two decades. With the ambitious Sam Hammam still in the chair, Cardiff could well become a force in the First Division.

# CARLISLE UNITED

## Brunton Park, Warwick Road, Carlisle, CA1 1LL

**Tel No:** 01228 526237
**Advance Tickets Tel No:** 01228 526237
**Fax:** 01228 530138
**Website:** www.carlisleunited.co.uk
**E-Mail:** admin@carlisleunited.co.uk
**League:** 3rd Division
**Brief History:** Founded 1904 as Carlisle United (previously named Shaddongate United). Former Grounds: Millholme Bank and Devonshire Park, moved to Brunton Park in 1909. Record attendance 27,500
**(Total) Current Capacity:** 13,655 (6,433 seated)
**Visiting Supporters' Allocation:** 2,000 (East Stand blocks 1 to 4)
**Club Colours:** Royal blue shirts, blue shorts

**Nearest Railway Station:** Carlisle Citadel
**Parking (Car):** Rear of ground
**Parking (Coach/Bus):** St Aiden's Road car park
**Police Force and Tel No:** Cumbria (01228 528191)
**Disabled Visitors' Facilities:**
  **Wheelchairs:** East Stand and Paddock (prior arrangement)
  **Blind:** No special facilities
**Anticipated Development(s):** Club owner John Courtenay announced in early June 2003 that the club's long-term future would include relocation but that there was no timescale envisaged.

### KEY

**C** Club Offices
**E** Entrance(s) for visiting supporters
**R** Refreshment bars for visiting supporters
**T** Toilets for visiting supporters

⬆ North direction (approx)

❶ A69 Warwick Road
❷ To M6 Junction 43
❸ Carlisle Citadel BR Station (1 mile)
❹ Greystone Road
❺ Car Park
❻ Petteril End (closed)

though Roddy Collins had, theoretically, departed from the United managerial hot seat at the end of the 2001/02 season, once the club's ownership was resolved he remained to guide the team through another season. Again, although the Cumbrians managed to guarantee their Third Division status for another year before the last day of the season, finishing in 22nd spot, one point above relegated Exeter City (with a vastly inferior goal difference), the threat of two-up/two-down with the Conference means that the Brunton Park faithful can look forward to another year of struggle against relegation in 2003/04. At the time of writing, despite threatening otherwise, Collins remains in position; if the season starts badly, however, it could lead to a change.

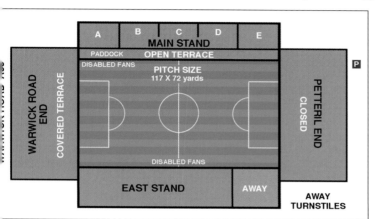

# CHARLTON ATHLETIC

## The Valley, Floyd Road, Charlton, London, SE7 8BL

**Tel No:** 020 8333 4000
**Advance Tickets Tel No:** 020 8333 4010
**Fax:** 020 8333 4001
**Web Site:** www.cafc.co.uk
**E-Mail:** info@cafc.co.uk
**League:** F.A. Premier
**Brief History:** Founded 1905. Former grounds: Siemens Meadows, Woolwich Common, Pound Park, Angerstein Athletic Ground, The Mount Catford, Selhurst Park (Crystal Palace FC), Boleyn Ground (West Ham United FC), The Valley (1912-23, 1924-85, 1992-date). Founder Members 3rd Division South. Record attendance 75,031
**(Total) Current Capacity:** 26,500 (all seated)
**Visiting Supporters' Allocation:** 3,000 (maximum; all seated in South Stand)

**Club Colours:** Red shirts, white shorts
**Nearest Railway Station:** Charlton
**Parking (Car):** Street parking
**Parking (Coach/Bus):** As directed by Police
**Police Force and Tel No:** Metropolitan (020 8853 8212)
**Disabled Visitors' Facilities:**
  **Wheelchairs:** East/West/South stands
  **Blind:** Commentary, 12 spaces
**Anticipated Development(s):** With completion of work on the North Stand the club is now looking to increase capacity to 36,000 through expansion of the East and South stands, although there is no confirmed timescale for the work

### KEY

**E** Entrance(s) for visiting supporters

**R** Refreshment bars for visiting supporters

**T** Toilets for visiting supporters

↑ North Direction (approx)

❶ Harvey Gardens
❷ A206 Woolwich Road
❸ Valley Grove
❹ Floyd Road
❺ Charlton BR Station
❻ East Stand
❼ North Stand
❽ West stand
❾ South stand (away)
❿ Charlton Church Lane
● Charlton Lane

*Above: 692147; Right: 692140*

curate's egg of a season for the Addicks' faithful saw the team alternate between good and bad
eriods with, at varying stages of the season, talk of either relegation or Europe. In the event, Alan
urbishley's team finished in the lower half of the table. Looking to the teams that are being promoted
om the First Division, none would seem likely to offer a serious threat to Charlton' continuing
survival at this level and 2003/04 should, therefore, see the team continue to consolidate its Premiership credentials.

# CHELSEA

## Stamford Bridge, Fulham Road, London, SW6 1HS

**Tel No:** 020 7385 5545
**Advance Tickets Tel No:** 020 7386 7799
**Fax:** 020 7381 4831
**Web Site:** www.chelseafc.com
**League:** F.A. Premier
**Brief History:** Founded 1905. Admitted to Football League (2nd Division) on formation. Stamford Bridge venue for F.A. Cup Finals 1919-22. Record attendance 82,905
**(Total) Current Capacity:** 42,449 (all seated)
**Visiting Supporters' Allocation:** Approx. 1,600 (East Stand Lower; can be increased to 3,200 if required or 5,200 if part of the Matthew Harding Stand [lower tier] is allocated)
**Club Colours:** Blue shirts, blue shorts

**Nearest Railway Station:** Fulham Broadway or West Brompton
**Parking (Car):** Street parking and underground car park at ground
**Parking (Coach/Bus):** As directed by Police
**Police Force and Tel No:** Metropolitan (020 7385 1212)
**Disabled Visitors' Facilities:**
  **Wheelchairs:** East Stand
  **Blind:** No special facility
**Anticipated Development(s):** With the long awaited completion of the second tier of the West Stand now achieved, redevelopment of Stamford Bridge as a stadium is now complete.

---

*KEY*

⬆ North direction (approx)

❶ A308 Fulham Road
❷ Central London
❸ To Fulham Broadway Tube Station
❹ Mathew Harding Stand
❺ East Stand
❻ West Stand
❼ South (Shed) Stand
❽ West Brompton Station

*Above: 688355; Right: 688356*

season, ultimately, of some limited success for Claudio Ranieri's squad could so easily have been a disaster except for the fact that the results on the last day of the season saw Chelsea pip Liverpool for the final Champions League position in a dramatic game at Stamford Bridge. With both teams level on points but with Chelsea having a superior goal difference, Liverpool needed to win to ensure another season in the Champions League. Whilst Chelsea could afford to draw, the team went one better and achieved a notable 2-1 victory. Whilst Champions League football has the potential to be a lucrative money-spinner, even in its revised format, the fact that the team failed again to maintain a serious challenge to the 'Big Two' will be a cause of concern to the Stamford Bridge faithful. Another season passed without a new entry into the club's collection of silverware and one wonders how long Ken Bates would have persevered with the current regime if he hadn't sold out to new Russian owners before the start of the campaign.

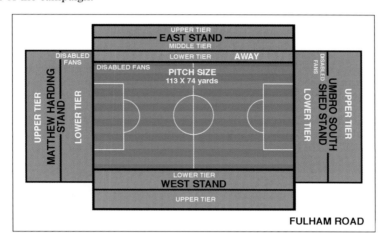

EAST STAND
UPPER TIER
MIDDLE TIER
LOWER TIER    AWAY

DISABLED FANS

DISABLED FANS

PITCH SIZE
113 X 74 yards

MATTHEW HARDING STAND
UPPER TIER    LOWER TIER

UMBRO SOUTH SHED STAND
DISABLED FANS    LOWER TIER    UPPER TIER

LOWER TIER
WEST STAND
UPPER TIER

FULHAM ROAD

# CHELTENHAM TOWN

## Whaddon Road, Cheltenham, Gloucestershire GL52 5NA

**Tel No:** 01242 573558
**Advance Tickets Tel No:** 01242 573558
**Fax:** 01242 224675
**Web Site:** www.cheltenhamtownfc.com
**E-Mail:** info@cheltenhamtownfc.com
**League:** 3rd Divison
**Brief History:** Cheltenham Town was founded in 1892. It moved to Whaddon Road in 1932 having previously played at Carter's Field. After two seasons in the Conference it achieved Nationwide League status at the end of the 1998/99 season. Record attendance 8,326
**(Total) Current Capacity:** 7,407 (3,139 seated)
**Visiting Supporters' Allocation:** 2,887 (maximum) in Whaddon Road Terrace – uncovered – and in Wymans Road Stand
**Club Colours:** Red and white striped shirts, white shorts

**Nearest Railway Station:** Cheltenham (1.5 miles)
**Parking (Car):** Limited parking at ground; otherwise on-street
**Parking (Coach/Bus):** As directed by Police
**Police Force and Tel No:** Gloucestershire (01242 521321)
**Disabled Visitors' Facilities:**
**Wheelchairs:** Six spaces in front of Main Stand
**Blind:** No special facility
**Anticipated Development(s):** The club plans to erect a cover over the Whaddon Road Terrace during the summer (unfortunately after the cut-off date for photography). This work will be followed by the construction of a new 5,000-seat main stand, although there is no confirmed date for the latter work.

**KEY**

**C** Club Offices
**E** Entrance(s) for visiting supporters

⬆ North direction (approx)

❶ B4632 Prestbury Road
❷ Cromwell Road
❸ Whaddon Road
❹ Wymans Road
❺ To B4075 Priors Road
❻ To B4075 Prior Road
❼ To Cheltenham town centre and railway station (1.5 and 2 miles respectively)
❽ Main Stand
❾ Wymans Road Stand
❿ Prestbury Road End
● Whaddon Road End

*Above:* 695569; *Right:* 695566

cing the new season at a higher level without Steve Cotterill was always going to be difficult for the
m and it was no surprise that the team struggled. With the Robins in the bottom four, new manager
aham Allner was sacked on 13 January. The club appointed a replacement manager quickly, with
perienced ex-Wales boss Bobby Gould being given the hot-seat until the end of the season. Under
management the team made a determined effort to beat the drop. In the event it all came down to
final Saturday as to whether Chesterfield or Cheltenham faced the drop. Unfortunately for the
bins a 1-0 defeat away at Notts County allied with Chesterfield's 1-1 draw at Blackpool sent the
bins back down to the Third Division. However, of all the teams relegated, Cheltenham is perhaps
best placed to make a serious challenge for promotion in 2003/04 and should reach the Play-Offs
worst.

# CHESTERFIELD

## Recreation Ground, Saltergate, Chesterfield, S40 4SX

**Tel No:** 01246 209765
**Advance Tickets Tel No:** 01246 209765
**Fax:** 01246 556799
**Web Site:** www.chesterfield-fc.co.uk
**E-Mail:** reception@cfc2.fsnet.co.uk
**League:** 2nd Division
**Brief History:** Found 1886. Former Ground: Spital Vale. Formerly named Chesterfield Town. Record attendance 30,968
**(Total) Current Capacity:** 8,300 (2,674 seated)
**Visiting Supporters' Allocation:** 2,200 maximum (maximum 800 seated)
**Club Colours:** Blue and white shirts, white shorts
**Nearest Railway Station:** Chesterfield

**Parking (Car):** Saltergate car park, street parking
**Parking (Coach/Bus):** As directed by Police
**Police Force and Tel No:** Derbyshire (01246 220100)
**Disabled Visitors' Facilities:**
**Wheelchairs:** Saltergate Stand
**Blind:** No special facility
**Anticipated Development(s):** Although the club has undertaken a lot of (very necessary) work on Saltergate in recent years, it is still uncertain as to whether it will seek to relocate to one of a number of possible sites identified or look to rebuild Saltergate. The final choice awaits a decision from the Chesterfield Supporters Association, the club's owners.

*KEY*

**C** Club Offices
**S** Club Shop
**E** Entrance(s) for visiting supporters
**R** Refreshment bars for visiting supporters
**T** Toilets for visiting supporters

⬆ North direction (approx)

❶ Saltergate
❷ Cross Street
❸ St Margaret's Drive
❹ West Bars
❺ To A617 & M1 Junction 29
❻ To station and town centre
❼ Compton Street Terrace
❽ Cross Street End (away)

*Above: 695552; Right: 695550*

With the Spireites one place above the Second Division drop-zone, Dave Rushbury departed from the managerial role at Saltergate at the end of April. The team's Second Division status was under threat ght until the last Saturday of the season, with a battle between the side and Cheltenham as to which am would face the drop. In the event, Chesterfield's 1-1 draw with Blackpool allied to Cheltenham's efeat at Notts County means that Second Division football will again be on offer at Saltergate in 003/04. However, the team will need to see a dramatic improvement if it isn't to feature again in the elegation battle although the new boss, the highly experienced Roy McFarland, does have the pedigree suggest that he will make a fight of it.

# COLCHESTER UNITED

## Layer Road Ground, Colchester, CO2 7JJ

**Tel No:** 0845 330 2975
**Advance Tickets Tel No:** 0845 330 2975
**Fax:** 01206 715327
**Web Site:** www.colchesterunited.net
**E-Mail:** sonya@colchesterunited.net
**League:** 2nd Division
**Brief History:** Founded 1937, joined Football League 1950, relegated 1990, promoted 1992. Record attendance 19,072
**(Total) Current Capacity:** 7,556 (1,877 seated)
**Visiting Supporters' Allocation:** 650 in Layer Road End (standing) plus 200 seats (East Coast Cable Stand)
**Club Colours:** Royal blue and white shirts, blue shorts
**Nearest Railway Station:** Colchester Town

**Parking (Car):** Street parking
**Parking (Coach/Bus):** Boadicea Way
**Police Force and Tel No:** Essex (01206 762212)
**Disabled Visitors' Facilities:**
  **Wheelchairs:** Space for 12 in front of terrace (next to Main Stand)
  **Blind:** Space for 3 blind persons and 3 guides (two regularly occupied by home supporters)
**Anticipated Development(s):** In the middle of April it was announced that the club's plans for relocation had received a boost with the Highway Authority giving the scheme the go-ahead. The new ground, to be located at the Cuckoo Farm site on the A12, is planned to provide a 10,000-all-seater capacity and, if all goes according to plan, will be opened for the start of the 2005/06 season.

### KEY

**C** Club Offices
**S** Club Shop
**E** Entrance(s) for visiting supporters
**R** Refreshment bars for visiting supporters
**T** Toilets for visiting supporters

↑ North direction (approx)

❶ B1026 Layer Road
❷ Town Centre & Colchester Town BR Station (2 miles)
❸ Evening Gazette Main Stand
❹ Barside Popular Side
❺ East Coast Cable Stand

wards the end of January, with United having dropped into the relegation zone with no wins in seven mes, manager Steve Whitton departed the Layer Road hot-seat after three and a half years in charge. fter a brief spell where Geraint Williams was in charge, the club appointed Phil Parkinson as its new anager towards the end of February. Under the new management, the team's fortunes improved measurably and, despite a final day defeat by QPR, the Us achieved a position of mid-table security, nishing in 12th with 58 points. Providing that the momentum can be maintained, then fans have every ason to be optimistic that 2003/04 will see the team consolidate further in the Second Division.

RAINSBOROWE ROAD

EVENING GAZETTE
MAIN STAND

TERRACE 3

COVERED SEATING

TERRACE 4

DISABLED ENCLOSURE
PITCH SIZE
110 x 70 yards

LAYER ROAD END
COVERED TERRACE

SECTION 2
AWAY

SECTION 1
AWAY

LAYER ROAD

EAST COAST
CABLE STAND

COVERED
SEATING

FAMILY
ENCLOSURE

E BLOCK
AWAY

PART COVERED TERRACE

FAMILY
ENCLOSURE

# COVENTRY CITY

## Highfield Road Stadium, King Richard Street, Coventry CV2 4FW

**Tel No:** 02476 234000
**Advance Tickets Tel No:** 02476 234020
**Fax:** 02476 234099
**Web Site:** www.ccfc.co.uk
**E-Mail:** info@ccfc.co.uk
**League:** 1st Division
**Brief History:** Founded 1883 as Singers F.C., changed name to Coventry City in 1898. Former grounds: Dowell's Field, Stoke Road Ground, moved to Highfield Road in 1899. Record attendance 51,455
**(Total) Current Capacity:** 23,627 all seated
**Visiting Supporters' Allocation:** 4,148 all seated in Mitchells & Butler Stand
**Club Colours:** Sky blue shirts, dark blue shorts
**Nearest Railway Station:** Coventry
**Parking (Car):** Street parking
**Parking (Coach/Bus):** Gosford Green Coach Park

**Police Force and Tel No:** West Midlands (02476 539010)
**Disabled Visitors' Facilities:**
  **Wheelchairs:** Clock Stand and East Stand
  **Blind:** Clock Stand (booking necessary)
**Anticipated Development(s):** The club, in conjunction with Coventry City Council (in Arena Coventry Ltd), is still progressing the new 32,500-seat ground at Foleshill at a cost of £60million. However, the original construction company has pulled out and will have to be replaced, putting in jeopardy the completion date (start of the 2004/05 season) although the club still hopes to commence construction in June 2003. Highfield Road has been sold for redevelopment and will disappear once the new ground is completed.

### KEY

- **C** Club Offices
- **S** Club Shop
- **E** Entrance(s) for visiting supporters
- **R** Refreshment bars for visiting supporters
- **T** Toilets for visiting supporters

↑ North direction (approx)

- ❶ Swan Lane
- ❷ Thackhall Street
- ❸ Nicholls Street
- ❹ Catherine Street
- ❺ A444 Phoenix Way
- ❻ Heath Road
- ❼ To M6 Junction 3
- ❽ To A428 Binley Road
- ❾ To Gosford Green coach park
- ❿ To Coventry station (one mile)
- ● M&B Stand

56

*Above:* 688720; *Right:* 688710

A number of ex-Premiership teams struggled to make an impact in the First Division in 2003/04 and Coventry was one of those that failed to make a mark in its second campaign at this level. Under tyro player-manager Gary McAllister the team gradually drifted down the table, finishing in 20th position only four points off the drop zone. Whilst the team's First Division status was never really under threat, the late surge by teams below them, such as Stoke and Sheffield Wednesday, must have made for uncomfortable viewing from Highfield Road. Unlike other ex-Premiership teams, such as Leicester and Ipswich, which descended into administration, the Sky Blues have battled through. However, the club's financial position means that the squad will be much reduced and, in what ought to prove the last season at Highfield Road before the move to the new ground, the team will have to perform much better it is to avoid being dragged into the relegation battle.

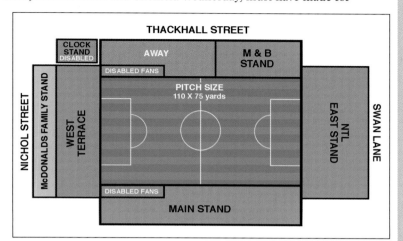

THACKHALL STREET

CLOCK STAND
DISABLED

AWAY

M & B STAND

DISABLED FANS

NICHOL STREET

McDONALDS FAMILY STAND

WEST TERRACE

PITCH SIZE
110 X 75 yards

NTL EAST STAND

SWAN LANE

DISABLED FANS

MAIN STAND

# CREWE ALEXANDRA

## The Alexandra Stadium, Gresty Road, Crewe, Cheshire, CW2 6EB

**Tel No:** 01270 213014
**Advance Tickets Tel No:** 01270 252610
**Fax:** 01270 216320
**Website:** www.crewealex.net
**E-Mail:** info@crewealex.net
**League:** 1st Division
**Brief History:** Founded 1877. Former Grounds: Alexandra Recreation Ground (Nantwich Road), Earle Street Cricket Ground, Edleston Road, Old Sheds Fields, Gresty Road (Adjacent to current Ground), moved to current Ground in 1906. Founder members of 2nd Division (1892) until 1896. Founder members of 3rd Division North (1921). Record attendance 20,000
**(Total) Current Capacity:** 10,100 all seated
**Visiting Supporters' Allocation:** 1,694 (BMW Stand)

**Club Colours:** Red shirts, white shorts
**Nearest Railway Station:** Crewe
**Parking (car):** There is a car park adjacent to the ground. It should be noted that there is a residents' only scheme in operation in the streets surrounding the ground.
**Parking (Coach/Bus):** As directed by Police
**Police Force and Tel No:** Cheshire (01270 500222)
**Disabled Visitors' Facilities:**
**Wheelchairs:** Available on all four sides
**Blind:** Commentary available
**Anticipated Development(s):** The club has long term plans for the construction of a new two-tier stand to replace the Ringways Stand, although there is no confirmed timescale for the work.

### KEY

**C** Club Offices
**S** Club Shop
**E** Entrance(s) for visiting supporters

↑ North direction (approx)

❶ Crewe BR Station
❷ Gresty Road
❸ Gresty Road
❹ A534 Nantwich Road
❺ To A5020 to M6 Junction 16
❻ To M6 Junction 17 [follow directions at roundabout to M6 J16/J17]
❼ Main Stand
❽ Gresty Road (Adtranz) Stand
❾ Railway End
❿ Ringways Stand (Blue Bell BMW)(away)
● Car Park

*Above:* 684966; *Right:* 684958

After the disappointment of the last-day relegation at the end of the 2001/02 season, the new campaign saw Dario Gradi's team continue to produce good football and the club was one of a number of teams chasing the second automatic promotion spot. For a long time it looked as though Cardiff City would sneak through, but the Railwaymen stuck well to their task and had promotion sewn up in the penultimate game of the season, thus making a last-day visit by rivals Cardiff City less of a strain than it might have proved. Crewe, on their day, proved themselves capable of matching virtually any team in the First Division when last at this level and with Gradi's ability to create a production line of new talent, hopes at Gresty Road will be high at the start of 2003/04. Like most promoted teams, the Railwaymen may well struggle initially, but a position mid-table should not be beyond the realms of possibility.

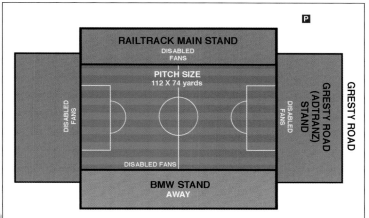

RAILTRACK MAIN STAND

DISABLED FANS

PITCH SIZE
112 X 74 yards

DISABLED FANS

DISABLED FANS

DISABLED FANS

GRESTY ROAD (ADTRANZ) STAND

GRESTY ROAD

P

BMW STAND
AWAY

# CRYSTAL PALACE

## Selhurst Park, London, SE25 6PU

**Tel No:** 020 8768 6000
**Advance Tickets Tel No:** 020 8771 8841
**Fax:** 020 8771 5311
**Web Site:** www.cpfc.co.uk
**E-Mail:** info@cpfc.co.uk
**Ticket Office/Fax:** 020 8653 4708
**League:** 1st Division
**Brief History:** Founded 1905. Former Grounds: The Crystal Palace (F.A. Cup Finals venue), London County Athletic Ground (Herne Hill), The Nest (Croydon Common Athletic Ground), moved to Selhurst Park in 1924. Founder members 3rd Division (1920). Record attendance 51,482
**(Total) Current Capacity:** 26,400 all seated
**Visiting Supporters' Allocation:** Approx 2,000 in Arthur Wait Stand
**Club Colours:** Blue and red striped shirts, red shorts

**Nearest Railway Station:** Selhurst, Norwood Junction and Thornton Heath
**Parking (Car):** Street parking and Sainsbury's car park
**Parking (Coach/Bus):** Thornton Heath
**Police Force and Tel No:** Metropolitan (020 8653 8568)
**Disabled Visitors' Facilities:**
  **Wheelchairs:** 56 spaces in Arthur Wait and Holmesdale Stands
  **Blind:** Commentary available
**Anticipated Development(s):** Although the club had plans to reconstruct the Main Stand — indeed had Planning Permission for the work — local opposition has meant that no work has been undertaken. Serious thought is now been given to relocation.

### KEY

**C** Club Offices
**S** Club Shop
**E** Entrance(s) for visiting supporters
**T** Toilets for visiting supporters

↑ North direction (approx)

❶ Whitehorse Lane
❷ Park Road
❸ A213 Selhurst Road
❹ Selhurst BR Station (¹/₂ mile)
❺ Norwood Junction BR Station (¹/₄ mile)
❻ Thornton Heath BR Station (¹/₂ mile)
❼ Car Park (Sainsbury's)

*Above:* 695773; *Right:* 695766

ch chairman Simon Jordan expressing displeasure with the squad's performance and with the team
ing to make a serious challenge even for the Play-Offs, it came as little surprise when Trevor Francis
arted from the Selhurst Park hot-seat at the end of April. Steve Kember took over on a temporary
is and guided the Eagles to a position of mid-table mediocrity. The one high point in the team's
otherwise disappointing season was victory at Anfield over Liverpool in the FA Cup. Steve Kember confirmed in his position during the summer will know that, in Simon Jordan, there is an ambitious chairman who will expect to see considerable progress on the field and the team making a serious challenge for the Premiership.

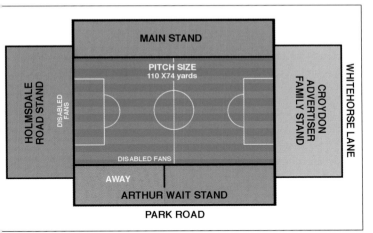

MAIN STAND

PITCH SIZE
110 X 74 yards

HOLMSDALE ROAD STAND

DISABLED FANS

DISABLED FANS

AWAY

ARTHUR WAIT STAND

PARK ROAD

CROYDON ADVERTISER FAMILY STAND

WHITEHORSE LANE

# DARLINGTON

## Neasham Road, Darlington

**Tel No:** 01325 240240*
**Advance Tickets Tel No:** 01325 242020*
**Fax:** 01325 240500*
* Note these are the numbers for Feethams; as the club will not be moving to the new ground until towards the end of 2002, these numbers should certainly be current for the first part of the season.
**Web Site:** www.darlington-fc.net
**E-mail:** alan_dfc@talk21.com
**League:** 3rd Division
**Brief History:** Founded 1883. Founder members of 3rd Division (North) 1921. Relegated from 4th Division 1989. Promoted from GM Vauxhall Conference in 1990. Previous Ground: Fathoms; moving to Neasham Road in 2003. Record attendance (at Feethams) 21,023
**(Total) Current Capacity:** 25,000

**Visiting Supporters' Allocation:** 3,000 in East Stand
**Club Colours:** White and black shirts, black shorts
**Nearest Railway Station:** Darlington Bank Top
**Parking (Car):** Spaces available in adjacent car park
**Parking (Coach/Bus):** As directed
**Police Force and Tel No:** Durham (01235 467681)
**Disabled Visitors Facilities:**
  **Wheelchairs:** 165 places
  **Blind:** tbc
**Anticipated Developments:** Despite pre-season expectations, the Quakers did not move to the new ground during the course of the 2002/03 season and, therefore, August 2003 will see the club finally make the move to Neasham Road.

↑ North direction (approx)

❶ A66
❷ To Stockton
❸ To A66(M) and A1(M)
❹ Neasham Road
❺ To Darlington town centre and railway station (one mile)
❻ To Neasham
❼ Snipe Lane

*Above:* 695517; *Right:* 695507

ter another disappointing start, Tommy Taylor was sacked as manager of the Quakers in late
ctober. His replacement, on a caretaker basis, was Mick Tait. Under Tait's stewardship, the club hit
d-table mediocrity, finishing in 14th position (albeit only six points off the drop zone). Whilst the
ub may well boast the best facilities in the Third Division, unless things improve dramatically on the
ld, it's hard to see the Quakers doing much more than struggle on the field and another battle
ainst the drop seems likely.

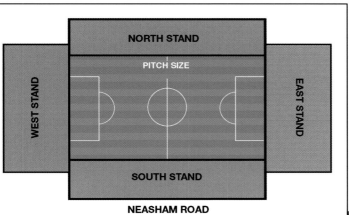

# DERBY COUNTY

## Pride Park, Derby, Derbyshire DE24 8XL

**Tel No:** 0870 444 1884
**Advance Tickets Tel No:** 0870 444 1884
**Fax:** 01332 667540
**Web Site:** www.dcfc.co.uk
**E-Mail:** derby.county@dcfc.co.uk
**League:** 1st Division
**Brief History:** Founded 1884. Former grounds: The Racecourse Ground, the Baseball Ground (1894-1997), moved to Pride Park 1997. Founder members of the Football League (1888). Record capacity at the Baseball Ground: 41,826; at Pride Park: 33,597
**(Total) Current Capacity:** 33,597
**Visiting Supporters' Allocation:** 4,800 in the South Stand
**Club Colours:** White shirts and black shorts

**Nearest Railway Station:** Derby
**Parking (Car):** 2,300 places at the ground designated for season ticket holders. Also two 1,000 car parks on the A6/A52 link road. No on-street parking
**Parking (Coach/Bus):** As directed
**Police Force and Tel No:** Derbyshire (01332 290100)
**Disabled Visitors' Facilities:**
    **Wheelchairs:** 70 home/30 away spaces
    **Blind:** Commentary available
**Anticipated Development(s):** There are no definite plans for the further development of Pride Park following the completion of the southwest corner.

**KEY**

**C** Club Offices
**S** Club Shop
**E** Entrance(s) for visiting supporters

↑ North direction (approx)

❶ To Derby Midland BR station
❷ North Stand
❸ Toyota West Stand
❹ South (McArthur Glen) Stand (away)
❺ Bombardier East Stand
❻ Derwent Parade
❼ To A52/M1
❽ To City Centre and A6
❾ A52

*Above:* 679691; *Right:* 679687

or a team that ought to have been challenging for an immediate return to the Premiership, 2002/03 as disastrous at Pride Park. Although the club avoided the Administration suffered by the other two ams relegated at the end of 2001/02, financial concerns were ever present and these were mpounded by problems off the field. Towards the end of the season, manager John Gregory was spended as a result of 'serious allegations' and ex-Ipswich boss George Burley was brought in to place him. Gregory would finally be dismissed, subject to appeal, shortly after the end of the season. nder Burley, the team — which at one point seemed to be heading rapidly towards a second ccessive relegation — saw its position stabilise and First Division football again guaranteed, although ast day 4-1 defeat at Pride Park by Ipswich Town showed how far the club had fallen. For 2003/04, urley, confirmed in his post after the end of the season, will have his work cut out to ensure that the am progresses. A number of good players have departed but those that are left — on the assumption that they're there to play football and not simply grasp the inflated Premiership-level salaries — ought to be good enough for a sustained challenge for promotion. However, the end of the season marks the end of the financial 'parachute' with all the consequences that this loss could entail.

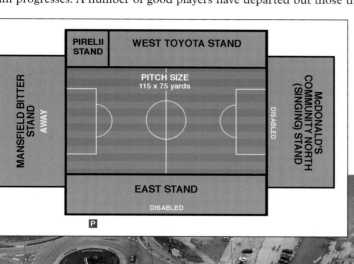

PIRELII STAND

WEST TOYOTA STAND

PITCH SIZE
115 x 75 yards

MANSFIELD BITTER STAND

AWAY

McDONALD'S COMMUNITY NORTH (SINGING) STAND

DISABLED

EAST STAND

DISABLED

P

# DONCASTER ROVERS

## Belle Vue, Bawtry Road, Doncaster, DN4 5HT

**Tel No:** 01302 539441
**Advance Tickets Tel No:** 01302 539441
**Fax:** 01302 539679
**Web Site:** www.doncasterroversfc.co.uk
**E-mail:** info@doncasterroversfc.co.uk
**League:** 3rd Division
**Brief History:** Founded 1879, Former grounds: Town Moor, Belle Vue (not current ground), Deaf School Playing Field (later name Intake Ground), Bennetthorpe, moved to Belle Vue (former name Low Pasture) in 1922. Returned to Football League after a five-year absence in 2003. Record attendance 37,149
**(Total) Current Capacity:** 7,600 (1,200 seated)

**Visiting Supporters' Allocation:** 1,204 on Rossington End terrace (open)
**Club Colours:** Red and white shirts, red shorts
**Nearest Railway Station:** Doncaster
**Parking (Car):** Car park at ground
**Parking (Coach/Bus):** Car park at ground
**Police Force and Tel No:** South Yorkshire (01302 366744)
**Disabled Visitors' facilities:**
  **Wheelchairs:** Bawtry Road
  **Blind:** No special facility
**Anticipated Development(s):** The club has plans to relocate but nothing is confirmed at this stage.

---

**KEY**

⬆ North direction (approx)

❶ Doncaster Racecourse
❷ A638 Bawtry Road
❸ To Bawtry
❹ To Doncaster town centre and railway station (1.5 miles)
❺ Carr House Road
❻ Car Park
❼ Main Stand
❽ Rossington End (away)

*Above: 695664; Right: 695660*

fter relegation from the Football League five years ago, Rovers initially struggled in the Conference.
owever, with the introduction of two-up/two-down the opportunity was there in 2002/03 for the
king. Although Yeovil dominated the division, a number of teams, including Rovers, were in the hunt
r the Play-Off places until towards the end when four — Rovers, Morecambe, Chester and
agenham — eased away from the chasing pack. In the semi-finals, Rovers defeated Chester, thereby
suring a final for Dave Penney's team against Dagenham & Redbridge at the Britannia Stadium.
hilst many neutrals have been favouring the Daggers, given the way that many felt that they had
en denied a Nationwide League place the previous year, football itself lacks sentiment. In the game
itself, Rovers took a 2-0 lead,
only to brought back to 2-2. In
extra time, played under the
'golden goal' rule, Rovers
scored again, in the 110th
minute, to restore Rovers'
football League status.
Promoted teams have generally
done reasonably well in the
Third Division; however, this is
the first occasion when a team
has been promoted through the
Play-Offs and it could well be
that a season of consolidation is
in order.

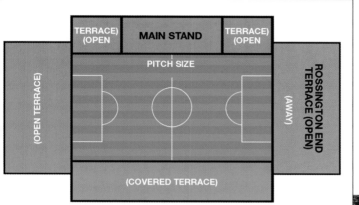

# EVERTON

## Goodison Park, Goodison Road, Liverpool, L4 4EL

**Tel No:** 0151 330 2200
**Advance Tickets Tel No:** 0151 330 2300
**Fax:** 0151 286 9112
**Web Site:** www.evertonfc.com
**E-Mail:** everton@evertonfc.com
**League:** F.A. Premier
**Brief History:** Founded 1879 as St. Domingo, changed to Everton in 1880. Former grounds: Stanley Park, Priory Road and Anfield (Liverpool F.C. Ground), moved to Goodison Park in 1892. Founder-members Football League (1888). Record attendance 78,299
**(Total) Current Capacity:** 40,170 all seated
**Visiting Supporters' Allocation:** 2,600 (part of Bullens Road Stand)
**Club Colours:** Blue and white shirts, white shorts
**Nearest Railway Station:** Liverpool Lime Street
**Parking (Car):** Corner of Utting Avenue and Priory Road

**Parking (Coach/Bus):** Priory Road
**Police Force and Tel No:** Merseyside (0151 709 6010)
**Disabled Visitors' Facilities:**
  **Wheelchairs:** Bullens Road Stand
  **Blind:** Commentary available
**Anticipated Development(s):** Towards the middle of April, it was announced that the club had pulled out of the King's Dock scheme, where it had been planned the club would occupy a new stadium. However, it was also announced that the club remained interested in relocation and would be discussing further options with Liverpool City council. Given the time frame involved with planning and redevelopment, it would appear that Everton will be remaining at Goodison for at least a couple of seasons.

| KEY | |
| --- | --- |
| **C** | Club Offices |
| **S** | Club Shop |
| **E** | Entrance(s) for visiting supporters |
| **R** | Refreshment bars for visiting supporters |
| **T** | Toilets for visiting supporters |

↑ North direction (approx)

❶ A580 Walton Road
❷ Bullen Road
❸ Goodison Road
❹ Car Park
❺ Liverpool Lime Street BR Station (2 miles)
❻ To M57 Junction 2, 4 and 5
❼ Stanley Park

*Above: 695687; Right: 695678*

After a number of seasons in which Everton were more concerned about events at the wrong end of the table, under David Moyes the Toffeemen were in the peculiar position of challenging for a spot in the UEFA Cup right up until the last Sunday of the season (indeed for much of the season it looked as though a spot in the Champions League was by no means impossible). In the event, however, a home defeat by Manchester United combined with Blackburn's demolition of Tottenham meant that European football will bypass Goodison for another season. It is a measure, however, of how far the team has progressed under Moyes that this will be regarded as a failure. In 2003/04, fans will undoubtedly expect more progress, although much will depend on the prodigious talent of Wayne Rooney. As an objective outsider, Everton's season could either be hugely successful or a major disappointment — the sensible money may well be on the latter as, amongst the top teams, Everton struggled most to score goals.

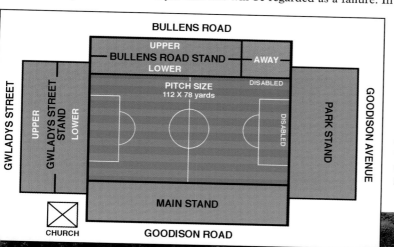

# FULHAM

## Loftus Road Stadium, South Africa Road, London, W12 7PA

**Club Offices:** Fulham Football Club Training Ground, Motspur Park, New Malden, Surrey KY3 6PT.
**Tel No:** 0870 442 1222
**Advance Tickets Tel No:** 0870 442 1234
**Fax:** 020 7384 4715
**Web Site:** www.fulhamfc.co.uk
**E-mail:** enquiries@fulham-fac.demon.co.uk
**League:** F.A. Premier
**Brief History:** Founded in 1879 as St. Andrews Fulham, changed name to Fulham 1897. Former Grounds: Star Road, Ranelagh Club, Lillie Road, Ell Brook Common, Purser's Cross, Barn Elms and Half Moon (Wasps Rugby Football ground), moved to Craven Cottage in 1894. Moved temporarily to Loftus Road in Autumn 2002. Record attendance (at Craven Cottage) 49,335
**(Total) Current Capacity:** 19,148
**Visiting Supporters' Allocation:** 3,100
**Club Colours:** White shirts, black shorts
**Nearest Railway Station:** Shepherds Bush and White City (both tube)

**Parking (Car):** White City NCP and street parking
**Parking (Coach/Bus):** White City NCP
**Police Force and Tel No:** Metropolitan (020 8246 7255)
**Disabled Visitors Facilities:**
**Wheelchairs:** Ellerslie Road Stand and West Paddock
  **Blind:** Ellerslie Road Stand
**Anticipated Developments:** The club's ambitious plans for the redevelopment of Craven Cottage have had to be scaled back and there is now no guarantee that this work will proceed or whether the club will return to its traditional home at all. If modernisation does take place then it will be much reduced from the original plans. Fulham will remain at Loftus Road for at least one more season. Another option for the future is to groundshare with Chelsea, but there are restrictive covenants on the use of Stamford Bridge resulting from the planning permission for the construction of the enlarged West Stand, which may preclude this.

### KEY

**C** QPR club offices
**S** QPR club shop
**E** Entrance(s) for visiting supporters

↑ North direction (approx)

❶ South Africa Road
❷ To White City Tube Station, A219 Wood Lane and A40 Western Avenue
❸ School End (away)
❹ South Africa Road Stand
❺ Loftus Road Stand
❻ Ellerslie Road Stand
❼ Loftus Road
❽ Bloemfontein Road
❾ Ellerslie Road

70

*Above: 695958; Right: 695954*

Towards the end of March it was announced that the club, after a period of uncertainty, would not be renewing the contract of Jean Tigana. However, a collapse in the team's form, perhaps the result of the uncertainty over the team's future direction, led to Tigana's departure at the end of April, with Chris Coleman taking over until the end of the season. Although Coleman stressed that he didn't feel that he was as yet ready to take the managerial role on full-time, the results that he achieved — which stabilised the team and ensured a 14th place finish (with three wins in the last five matches) — encouraged chairman Mohamed al-Fayed to think that Coleman might offer a better option than many of the touted alternatives. In mid-May it was announced that Coleman had taken on the position, but he will, however, face a real challenge in keeping the Cottagers in the Premiership, wherever they end up playing in 2004/05.

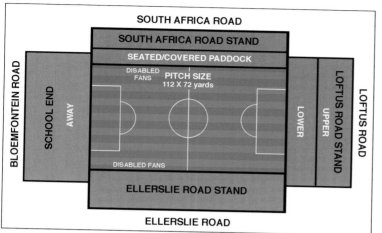

SOUTH AFRICA ROAD

SOUTH AFRICA ROAD STAND

SEATED/COVERED PADDOCK

DISABLED FANS

PITCH SIZE
112 X 72 yards

BLOEMFONTEIN ROAD

SCHOOL END

AWAY

DISABLED FANS

ELLERSLIE ROAD STAND

ELLERSLIE ROAD

LOFTUS ROAD STAND

LOWER

UPPER

LOFTUS ROAD

# GILLINGHAM

## Priestfield Stadium, Redfern Avenue, Gillingham, Kent, ME7 4DD

**Tel No:** 01634 300000
**Advance Tickets Tel No:** 01634 851854
**Fax:** 01634 300000
**Web Site:** www.gillinghamfootballclub.com
**E-mail:** info@gillinghamfootballclub.com
**League:** 1st Division
**Brief History:** Founded 1893, as New Brompton, changed name to Gillingham in 1913. Founder-members Third Division (1920). Lost Football League status (1938), re-elected to Third Division South (1950). Record attendance 23,002
**(Total) Current Capacity:** 11,582 (7,822 seated)
**Visiting Supporters' Allocation:** 1,300 (in Redfern Terrace Avenue Corner Terrace)
**Club Colours:** Blue and black hooped shirts, blue shorts
**Nearest Railway Station:** Gillingham

**Parking (Car):** Street parking
**Parking (Coach/Bus):** As directed by Police
**Police Force and Tel No:** Kent (01634 234488)
**Disabled Visitors' Facilities:**
  **Wheelchairs:** Redfern Avenue (Main) Stand
  **Blind:** No special facility
**Anticipated Development(s):** Planning permission was granted for the construction of the new stand towards the end of April 2003. Construction, however, may be delayed for up to a year. This work will involve the replacement of the existing Town End Terrace with a new 3,500-seat structure. However, despite the work that has been undertaken at the Priestfield Stadium, chairman Paul Scally is still looking in the long term to relocate. One site that has been identified is at Temple Marshes, but at this stage nothing is confirmed.

### KEY

**E** Entrance(s) for visiting supporters

↑ North direction (approx)

❶ Redfern Avenue
❷ Toronto Road
❸ Gordon Road
❹ Gillingham BR station (1/4 mile)
❺ Gordon Street Stand
❻ New two-tier Main (Medway) Stand
❼ New Rainham End Stand
❽ Gillingham End; uncovered terrace

*Above:* 692151; *Right:* 692159

GORDON ROAD

**GORDON ROAD STAND**

PITCH SIZE
114 X 75 yards

TORONTO ROAD

RAINHAM END STAND

GILLINGHAM END UNCOVERED TERRACE

PRIESTFIELD ROAD

AWAY

DISABLED FANS

LOWER

**MAIN MEDWAY STAND**

UPPER

REDFERN AVENUE

Under Andy Hessenthaler — who will hang up his playing boots at the end of the season to concentrate upon his managerial role — the Gills again achieved a position of mid-table safety in the First Division, finishing in 11th some 12 points off the Play-Off spots. Now that the team's position in the First Division has been secured, fans will be expecting the side to make a serious challenge for the Play-Offs at least in 2003/04.

# GRIMSBY TOWN

## Blundell Park, Cleethorpes, DN35 7PY

**Tel No:** 01472 605050
**Advance Tickets Tel No:** 01472 605050
**Fax:** 01472 693665
**Web Site:** www.gtfc.co.uk
**E-Mail:** enquiries@gtfc.co.uk
**League:** 2nd Division
**Brief History:** Founded in 1878, as Grimsby Pelham, changed name to Grimsby Town in 1879. Former Grounds: Clee Park (two adjacent fields) and Abbey Park, moved to Blundell Park in 1899. Founder-members 2nd Division (1892). Record attendance 31,651
**(Total) Current Capacity:** 10,033 (all seated)
**Visiting Supporters' Allocation:** 2,200 in Osmond Stand
**Club Colours:** Black and white striped shirts, black shorts
**Nearest Railway Station:** Cleethorpes

**Parking (Car):** Street parking
**Parking (Coach/Bus):** Harrington Street
**Police Force and Tel No:** Humberside (01472 359171)
**Disabled Visitors' Facilities:**
  **Wheelchairs:** Harrington Street (Main) Stand
  **Blind:** Commentary available
**Anticipated Development(s):** The club's plans for relocation took a hit in mid-April when it appeared that the local council was likely to throw out the planning application. If it progresses, the club's plans envisage the construction of a new £14million stadium at Great Coates with an anticipated capacity of 14,000 all-seated. A sponsorship deal has been put in place that will see the ground named after the oil company Conoco.

### KEY

**C** Club Offices
**S** Club Shop
**E** Entrance(s) for visiting supporters
**R** Refreshment bars for visiting supporters
**T** Toilets for visiting supporters

↑ North direction (approx)

❶ A180 Grimsby Road
❷ Cleethorpes BR Station (1½ miles)
❸ To Grimsby and M180 Junction 5
❹ Harrington Street
❺ Constitutional Avenue
❻ Humber Estuary

e of a number of teams involved in the relegation dog fight right from the start of the season, imsby were in the bottom three virtually throughout the season and it came as little surprise that al Groves's team ultimately succumbed. When last relegated the Mariners made a pretty prompt urn to the First Division and there must be every chance that a similar result will occur. The team uld have the potential to mount a challenge for the Play-Offs at the worst.

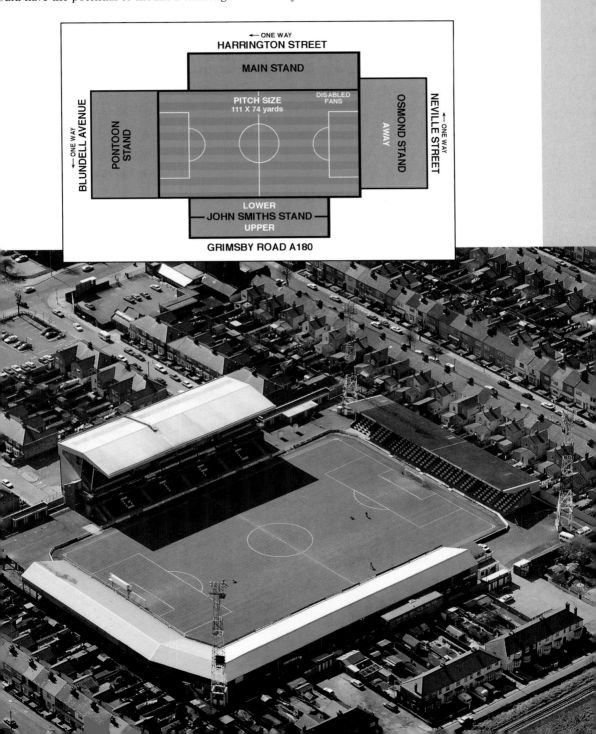

# HARTLEPOOL UNITED

## Victoria Park, Clarence Road, Hartlepool, TS24 8BZ

**Tel No:** 01429 272584
**Advance Tickets Tel No:** 01429 272584
**Fax:** 01429 863007
**Web Site:** www.hartlepoolunited.co.uk
**E-Mail:** info@hartlepoolunited.co.uk
**Fax:** 01429 863007
**League:** 2nd Division
**Brief History:** Founded 1808 as Hartlepools United, changed to Hartlepool (1968) and to Hartlepool United in 1977. Founder-members 3rd Division (1921). Record attendance 17,426
**(Total) Current Capacity:** 7,629 (3,966 seated)
**Visiting Supporters' Allocation:** 720 (located in Rink Stand)
**Club Colours:** Blue and white striped shirts, blue shorts

**Nearest Railway Station:** Hartlepool Church Street
**Parking (Car):** Street parking and rear of clock garage
**Parking (Coach/Bus):** As directed
**Police Force and Tel No:** Cleveland (01429 221151
**Disabled Visitors' Facilities:**
  **Wheelchairs:** Cyril Knowles Stand and Rink End
  **Blind:** Commentary available
**Anticipated Development(s):** The plans for the redevelopment of the Millhouse Stand are still progressing, although there is now no definite timescale. When this work does commence, the ground's capacity will be reduced to 5,000 temporarily.

**KEY**

**C** Club Offices
**S** Club Shop
**E** Entrance(s) for visiting supporters

↑ North direction (approx)

❶ A179 Clarence Road
❷ Hartlepool Church Street BR Station
❸ Marina Way
❹ Site of former Greyhound Stadium
❺ To Middlesbrough A689 & A1(M)
❻ To A19 North
❼ Rink End Stand

*Above: 695504; Right: 695500*

llowing the departure of Chris Turner, who moved to take over at Sheffield Wednesday in early vember with the team top of the Third Division, Mike Newell was appointed manager on November. Despite the loss of Turner, the team continued to perform well and automatic motion to the Second Division was achieved. The championship, however, went right to the wire h the two contenders — United and Rushden — meeting at Nene Park. In the event, a 1-1 draw s sufficient to give the title to the ambitious Northamptonshire team by two points. Ironically, ited will renew contact with ex-boss Turner in 2003/04 as his Wednesday team was relegated. As

with all promoted teams, the new campaign could prove a struggle as the team looks to consolidate at a higher level. Curiously, despite his success in taking the club into the Second Division, Newell's contract was not renewed at the end of May and so the team will face the daunting prospect of playing at a higher level with a new man, Neale Cooper, in charge.

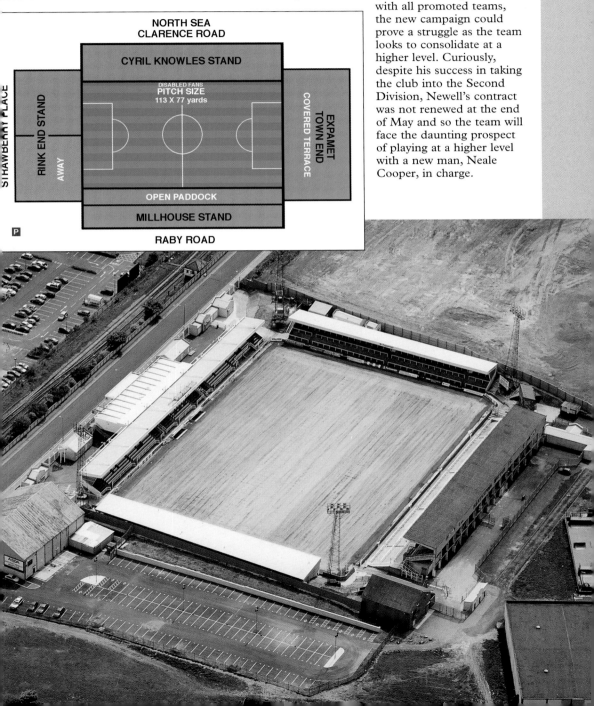

**NORTH SEA**
**CLARENCE ROAD**

**CYRIL KNOWLES STAND**

DISABLED FANS
**PITCH SIZE**
113 X 77 yards

STRAWBERRY PLACE

**RINK END STAND**

AWAY

EXPAMET
TOWN END
COVERED TERRACE

**OPEN PADDOCK**

**MILLHOUSE STAND**

**RABY ROAD**

# HUDDERSFIELD TOWN

## The Alfred McAlpine Stadium, Leeds Road, Huddersfield, HD1 6PX

**Tel No:** 01484 484100
**Advance Tickets Tel No:** 01484 484123
**Fax:** 01484 484101
**Web Site:** www.htafc.com
**League:** 3rd Division
**Brief History:** Founded 1908, elected to Football League in 1910. First Club to win the Football League Championship three years in succession. Moved from Leeds Road ground to Kirklees (Alfred McAlpine) Stadium 1994/95 season. Record attendance (Leeds Road) 67,037; McAlpine Stadium: 23,678
**(Total) Current Capacity:** 24,500 (all seated)
**Visiting Supporters' Allocation:** 4,037 (all seated)
**Club Colours:** Blue and white striped shirts , white shorts

**Nearest Railway Station:** Huddersfield
**Parking (Car):** Car parks (pre-sold) adjacent to ground
**Parking (Coach/Bus):** Car parks adjacent to ground
**Police Force and Tel No:** West Yorkshire (01484 422122)
**Disabled Visitors' Facilities:**
　**Wheelchairs:** Three sides of Ground, at low levels and raised area, including toilet access
　**Blind:** Area for Partially sighted with Hospital Radio commentary
**Anticipated Development(s):** With completion of the new North Stand, work on the McAlpine Stadium is over.

---

### KEY
**C** Club Offices
**S** Club Shop
**E** Entrance(s) for visiting supporters

↑ North direction (approx)

❶ To Leeds and M62 Junction 25
❷ A62 Leeds Road
❸ To Huddersfield BR station (1¼ miles)
❹ Disabled parking
❺ Town Avenue pay car park (on site of former ground)
❻ North Stand
❼ St Andrews pay car park
❽ Coach park
❾ South Stand (away)

*Above: 695676; Right: 695671*

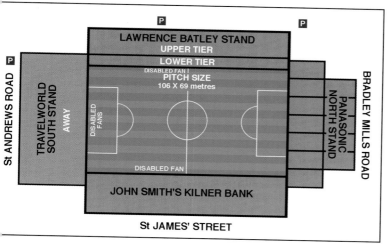

With the Terriers rooted to the bottom of the Second Division, having gained one point in the previous matches, Mick Wadsworth was sacked on 26 March; he was replaced, on a caretaker basis, by ex-Bournemouth boss Mel Machin. Unfortunately, the experienced Machin — handicapped by the club's financial problems — was unable to string enough good results together with the result that the Terriers find themselves in the Third Division for 2003/04. At the end of the season, the administrators acted to reduce further the staffing at the club, resulting in Machin's departure. At the time of writing the club had just appointed Peter Jackson as manager.

# HULL CITY

## Kingston Communications Stadium, Walton Street, Hull, East Yorkshire HU3 6HU

**Tel No:** 0870 837 0003
**Advance Tickets Tel No:** 0870 837 0004
**Fax:** 01482 304882
**Web Site:** www.hullcityafc.net
**E-mail:** info@hulltigers.com
**League:** 3rd Division
**Brief History:** Founded 1904. Former grounds: The Boulevard (Hull Rugby League Ground), Dairycoates, Anlaby Road Cricket Circle (Hull Cricket Ground), Anlaby Road, Boothferry Park (from 1946). Moved to Kingston Communications Stadium in late 2002. Record attendance (at Boothferry Park) 55,019; (at Kingston Communications Stadium) 22,319
**(Total) Current Capacity:** 25,404 (all-seated)
**Visiting Supporters' Allocation:** 4,000 all-seated in North Stand
**Club Colours:** Amber with black and white trim shirts, black shorts

**Nearest Railway Station:** Hull Paragon
**Parking (Car):** There are 1,800 spaces on the Walton Street Fairground for use on match days
**Parking (Coach/Bus):** As directed
**Police Force and Tel No:** Humberside (01482 220148)
**Disabled Visitors' facilities:**
  **Wheelchairs:** tbc
  **Blind:** tbc
**Anticipated Development(s):** The club moved into the new Kingston Communication Stadium towards the end of 2002. The ground is shared with Hull RLFC. The total cost of the 25,404-seat ground was £44million. The West Stand is provided with two tiers and there are plans for the construction of a second tier on the East Stand, taking the capacity to 30,000, if required.

### KEY

⬆ North direction (approx)

❶ A1105 Anlaby Road
❷ Arnold Lane
❸ West Stand
❹ East Stand
❺ Walton Street
❻ To city centre and railway station
❼ Car parks
❽ Railway line towards Scarborough
❾ Railway line towards Leeds
❿ A1105 westwards towards A63 and M62

*Above:* 695565; *Right:* 695561

After a highly disappointing start to the new season, Jan Molby was sacked as manager on 11 October 2002. The club moved quickly to appoint a replacement, with erstwhile Gillingham, Brighton and Leicester boss Peter Taylor taking over on the following day. Under Taylor, City achieved a position of mid-table mediocrity, although the new stadium certainly encouraged the faithful to turn out in greater numbers than before. However, Taylor's conservative approach to the game has not proved hugely popular with the fans. With the team's average gate well above the norm for the Third Division, with the extra financial clout that this offers in the now financially-challenged Nationwide League, City should be one of the pre-season favourites for promotion. Failure to make a sustained bid for promotion will undoubtedly lead to more pressure on the manager.

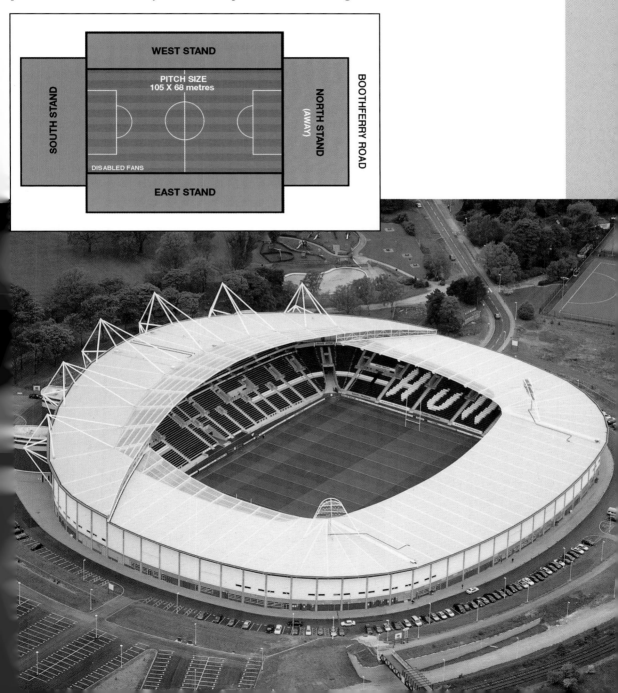

# IPSWICH TOWN

## Portman Road, Ipswich, IP1 2DA

**Tel No:** 01473 400500
**Advance Tickets Tel No:** 01473 4000555
**Fax:** 01473 400040
**Web Site:** http://www.itfc.co.uk
**E-Mail:** enquiries@itfc.co.uk
**League:** 1st Division
**Brief History:** Founded 1887 as Ipswich Association F.C., changed to Ipswich Town in 1888. Former Grounds: Broom Hill & Brookes Hall, moved to Portman Road in 1888. Record attendance 38,010
**(Total) Current Capacity:** 30,326 all seated
**Visiting Supporters' Allocation:** 1,771 all seated in Cobbold Stand
**Club Colours:** Blue shirts, white shorts
**Nearest Railway Station:** Ipswich

**Parking (Car):** Portman Road, Portman Walk & West End Road
**Parking (Coach/Bus):** West End Road
**Police Force and Tel No:** Suffolk (01473 611611)
**Disabled Visitors' Facilities:**
  **Wheelchairs:** Lower Britannia Stand
  **Blind:** Commentary available
**Anticipated Development(s):** The new Greene King (South) Stand has been followed by the construction of the new two-tier, 7,035-seat, North Stand, which was initially delayed as a result of legal action. The completion of the two stands takes Portman Road's capacity to more than 30,000.

---

### KEY

**C** Club Offices
**E** Entrance(s) for visiting supporters
**R** Refreshment bars for visiting supporters
**T** Toilets for visiting supporters

↑ North direction (approx)

❶ A137 West End Road
❷ Sir Alf Ramsay Way
❸ Portman Road
❹ Princes Street
❺ To Ipswich BR Station
❻ Car Parks
❼ Cobbold Stand
❽ Britannia Stand
❾ North Stand
❿ Greene King (South) Stand

*Above:* 694286; *Right:* 694275

Although retaining the bulk of the squad from the Premiership, Ipswich's domestic season started disastrously and, following a heavy defeat at relegation threatened Grimsby Town, George Burley was sacked on 12 October. With the club seeking a quick replacement, Tony Mowbray took over on a caretaker basis. After several names were mentioned as possibilities, Joe Royle emerged to take over. Whilst the appointment did not meet with universal approval by fans, Royle did ensure that the club's progress in the UEFA cup continued further than many had expected and also brought sufficient points in the First Division to mount a meaningful challenge for the Play-Offs, but, in the event, the points lost earlier in the season handicapped the team towards the end, with the result that Tractorboys finished in seventh place, four points adrift of Nottingham Forest. Although the club is now out of Administration, the likelihood is that more high-profile players will depart, thus making the new season again one of considerable challenge. However, despite the departees, Royle should have enough talent left in the squad to ensure that the early season failures of 2002/03 are not repeated.

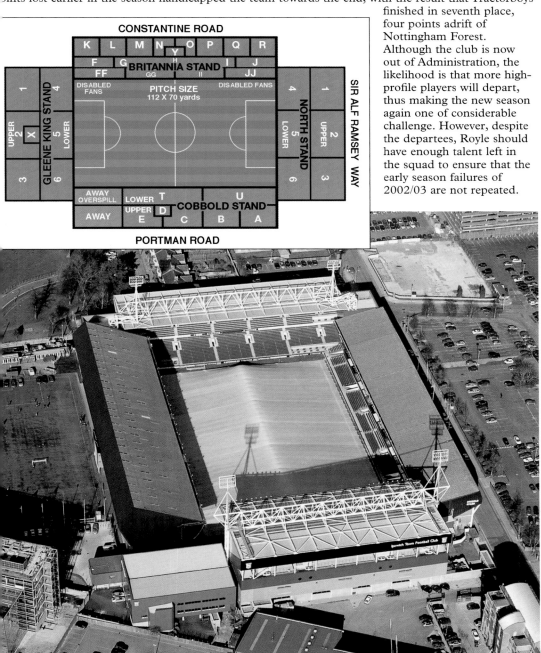

# KIDDERMINSTER HARRIERS

## Aggborough Stadium, Hoo Road, Kidderminster, Worcestershire DY10 1NB

**Tel No:** 01562 823931
**Advance Tickets Tel No:** 01562 823931
**Fax:** 01562 827329
**Web Site:** www.harriers.co.uk
**E-Mail:** info@harriers.co.uk
**League:** 3rd Division
**Brief History:** The club was established in 1886. There have been no previous grounds. The team won the Nationwide Conference title at the end of the 1999/2000 season and entered the Nationwide League for 2000/01 season. Record attendance at Aggborough Stadium: 9,155
**(Total) Current Capacity:** 6,293 (3,150 seated)
**Visiting Supporters' Allocation:** 1,500 (all unseated in South [College End] Terrace), plus up to 760 seated in new East (William Greaves) Stand

**Club Colours:** Red shirts with white markings; red shorts
**Nearest Railway Station:** Kidderminster
**Parking (Car):** Limited at ground parking otherwise on-street
**Parking (Coach/Bus):** As directed
**Police Force and Tel No:** West Mercia (01562 820888
**Disabled Visitors' Facilities:**
**Wheelchairs:** Designated section in front of George Reynolds Stand
**Blind:** No special facility
**Anticipated Development(s):** The Bill Greaves Terrace ceased to be in mid-February 2003. It will be replaced by a new all-seater stand, accommodating 2,040, by the start of the new season.

### KEY

**C** Club Offices
**S** Club Shop
**E** Entrance(s) for visiting supporters

⬆ North direction (approx)

❶ South (College) End – away
❷ Kidderminster Town station (Severn Valley Railway)
❸ Kidderminster station
❹ Hoo Road
❺ Constitution Hill Ringway
❻ To Town Centre (half a mile)
❼ Chester Road South
❽ To A449 and M5 (14 miles)
❾ Stadium Close
❿ Car park
⓫ Harriers Trading Estate
⓬ Vicarage Close

*Above:* 695596; *Right:* 695602

r Ian Britton, who had taken over the reins at Aggborough towards the end of the 2001/02
n, Harriers were always a top half of Division Three team without ever threatening to get into
r one of the automatic promotion spots nor the Play-Offs. Ultimately, the team finished in 11th
ion some seven points below the Play-Off zone. For 2003/04 fans will be expecting the team to
significant progress towards promotion, although it's hard to escape the conclusion that another
n of mid-table mediocrity beckons.

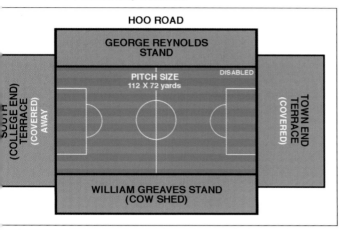

**HOO ROAD**

**GEORGE REYNOLDS STAND**

DISABLED

**PITCH SIZE**
112 X 72 yards

SOUTH (COLLEGE END) TERRACE (COVERED) AWAY

TOWN END TERRACE (COVERED)

**WILLIAM GREAVES STAND (COW SHED)**

# LEEDS UNITED

## Elland Road, Leeds, LS11 0ES

**Tel No:** 0113 367 6000
**Advance Tickets Tel No:** 0845 121 1992
**Fax:** 0113 367 6050
**Web Site:** www.leedsunited.com
**E-mail:** admin@leedsunited.com
**League:** F.A. Premier
**Brief History:** Founded 1919, formed from the former 'Leeds City' Club, who were disbanded following expulsion from the Football League in October 1919. Joined Football League in 1920. Record attendance 57,892
**(Total) Current Capacity:** 40,296 (all seated)
**Visiting Supporters' Allocation:** 1,725 in South East Corner (can be increased to 3,662 in South Stand if necessary)
**Club Colours:** White shirts, white shorts

**Nearest Railway Station:** Leeds City
**Parking (Car):** Car parks adjacent to ground
**Parking (Coach/Bus):** As directed by Police
**Police Force and Tel No:** West Yorkshire (0113 243 5353)
**Disabled Visitors' Facilities:**
　**Wheelchairs:** West Stand and South Stand
　**Blind:** Commentary available
**Anticipated Development(s):** The club has plans for the construction of a new £60m 50,000-seat ground — part funded through the sale of Elland Road — to be built for start of 2005/06 season. Although the actual site for the new ground has yet to be confirmed, the club has been investigating a location close to the A1/M1 link road.

---

### KEY

**C** Club Offices
**S** Club Shop
**E** Entrance(s) for visiting supporters

↑ North direction (approx)

❶ M621
❷ M621 Junction 2
❸ A643 Elland Road
❹ Lowfields Road
❺ To A58
❻ City Centre and BR station
❼ To M62 and M1

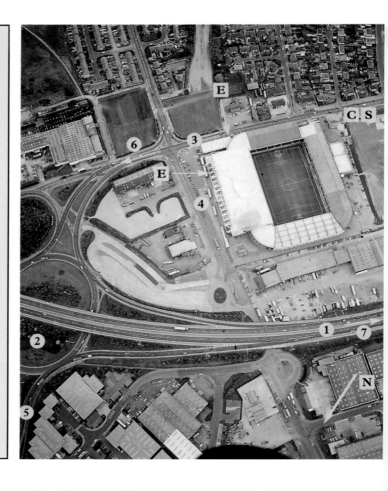

Last season was probably a season that most United fans would prefer to forget. On the field, Terry Venables' team rarely performed up to the level of a squad that he inherited at the start of the season and pressure on the manager grew throughout the campaign. With Leeds still seriously threatened by relegation, Venables departed from the hot seat, to be followed shortly afterwards by the club's high-profile chairman, Peter Ridsdale, as the extent of the club's financial problems became clear. Ex-Sunderland boss, Peter Reid, was brought in to steady the ship and Premiership survival was assured with an away win at Arsenal in the penultimate game of the season. Reid's reward was a new rolling one-year contract and the hope that 2003/04 will prove more successful on the field. However, the new manager inherited a squad already shorn of many talented players — such as Jonathan Woodgate and Lee Bowyer — with others likely to depart as the club's new board make a serious attempt to turn the team's financial fortunes around.

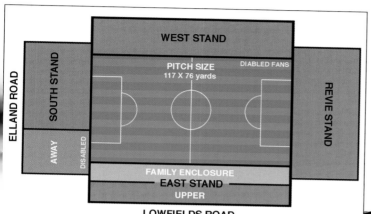

WEST STAND

PITCH SIZE
117 X 76 yards

DIABLED FANS

ELLAND ROAD

SOUTH STAND

AWAY

DISABLED

REVIE STAND

FAMILY ENCLOSURE
EAST STAND
UPPER

LOWFIELDS ROAD

# LEICESTER CITY

## Walkers Stadium, Filbert Way, Leicester, LE2 7FL

**Tel No:** 0870 040 6000
**Advance Tickets Tel No:** 0870 040 6000
**Fax:** 0116 229 4404
**Web Site:** www.lcfc.co.uk
**E-mail:** ticket.sales@lcfc.co.uk
**League:** F.A. Premiership
**Brief History:** Founded 1884 at Leicester Fosse, changed name to Leicester City in 1919. Former grounds: Fosse Road South, Victoria Road, Belgrave Cycle Track, Mill Lane, Aylstone Road Cricket Ground and Filbert Street (from 1891). The club moved to the new Walkers Stadium for the start of the 2002/03 season. Record attendance (at Filbert Street) 47,298; (at Walkers Stadium) 32,082
**(Total) Current Capacity:** 32,500
**Visiting Supporters' Allocation:** 3,000 (all seated) in North East of Ground

**Club Colours:** Blue shirts, white shorts
**Nearest Railway Station:** Leicester
**Parking (Car):** NCP car park
**Parking (Coach/Bus):** As directed
**Police Force and Tel No:** Leicester (0116 222 2222)
**Disabled Visitors Facilities:**
  **Wheelchairs:** 186 spaces spread through all stands
  **Blind:** Match commentary via hospital radio
**Anticipated Developments:** The club moved into the new 32,500-seat Walkers Stadium at the start of the 2002/03 season. Although there are no plans at present, the stadium design allows for the construction of a second tier to the East Stand, taking capacity to 40,000.

---

**KEY**

**C** Club Offices

⬆ North direction (approx)

❶ Raw Dykes Road
❷ Eastern Road
❸ A426 Aylstone Road
❹ Freeman's Common Road
❺ To Lutterworth
❻ To city centre and railway station (one mile)
❼ Burnmoor Street
❽ River Soar
❾ Site of Filbert Street (old ground)

*Above:* 695615; *Right:* 695611

first season at the new ground should have been one of unmitigated success for City, but the
ing was overshadowed by the team's relegation to the First Division and then by the club's well-
cised collapse into Administration. However, despite the off-the-field problems, on the field
ey Adams managed to retain the majority of the squad from 2001/02 and therefore was able to
it a sustained challenge for automatic promotion. In the event, although the championship was
nd the team, automatic promotion was assured and Premiership football will arrive at the Walkers
um in 2003/04. Off the field, the Gary Lineker-led consortium saw the team emerge from
inistration. However, given the financial circumstances that the club finds itself in, it is hard not to
he Foxes as one of the favourites for relegation.

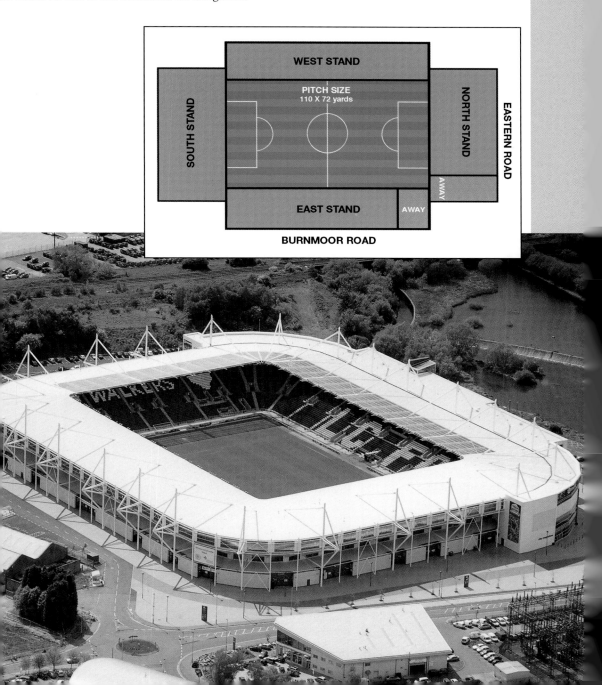

# LEYTON ORIENT

## Matchroom Stadium, Brisbane Road, Leyton, London, E10 5NF

**Tel No:** 020 8926 1111
**Advance Tickets Tel No:** 020 8926 1010
**Fax:** 020 8926 1110
**Web Site:** www.leytonorient.com
**E-Mail:** info@leytonorient.net
**League:** 3rd Division
**Brief History:** Founded 1887 as Clapton Orient, from Eagle Cricket Club (formerly Glyn Cricket Club formed in 1881). Changed name to Leyton Orient (1946), Orient (1966), Leyton Orient (1987). Former grounds: Glyn Road, Whittles Athletic Ground, Millfields Road, Lea Bridge Road, Wembley Stadium (2 games), moved to Brisbane Road in 1937. Record attendance 34,345
**(Total) Current Capacity:** 11,127 (7,027 seated)
**Visiting Supporters' Allocation:** 1,500 (all seated) in East Stand/Terrace

**Club Colours:** Red shirts, red shorts
**Nearest Railway Station:** Leyton (tube), Leyton Midland Road
**Parking (Car):** Street parking
**Parking (Coach/Bus):** As directed by Police
**Police Force and Tel No:** Metropolitan (020 8556 8855)
**Disabled Visitors' Facilities:**
  **Wheelchairs:** Windsor Road
  **Blind:** Match commentary supplied on request
**Anticipated Development(s):** The club's proposals for the redevelopment of the West Stand and North Terrace were approved by the local council in mid-May. The £9million scheme, aimed eventually to give the stadium a capacity of 10,500, will be funded largely by the construction of residential apartments at the four corners of the ground by Bellway Homes.

### KEY

**C** Club Offices
**S** Club Shop
**E** Entrance(s) for visiting supporters

↑ North direction (approx)

❶ Buckingham Road
❷ Oliver Road
❸ A112 High Road Leyton
❹ To Leyton Tube Station (¼ mile)
❺ Brisbane Road
❻ Windsor Road
❼ To Leyton Midland Road BR station
❽ South Stand

*Above:* 695640; *Right:* 695637

London's only team in the Football League's basement division had a disappointing season, with Paul Brush's team failing to make progress in the FA Cup — being defeated by non-league Margate 1-0 in a First Round replay — and finishing a disappointing 18th in the league, only five points above the drop zone. With the two-up/two-down principle now firmly established, unless the team's form improves dramatically in 2003/04 it is hard to escape the conclusion that Orient will be more concerned with events at the bottom of the table than the pursuit of promotion.

OLIVER ROAD

WEST STAND

PITCH SIZE
115 X 80 yards

BUCKINGHAM ROAD

SOUTH STAND

NORTH TERRACE
UNCOVERED

WINDSOR ROAD

DISABLED FANS

AWAY ENCLOSURE

ENCLOSURE

WINGS

AWAY SEATS

EAST STAND

BRISBANE ROAD

# LINCOLN CITY

## Sincil Bank, Lincoln, LN5 8LD

**Tel No:** 01522 880011
**Advance Tickets Tel No:** 01522 880011
**Fax:** 01522 880020
**Web Site:** www.redimps.com
**E-Mail:** lcfc@redimps.com
**League:** 3rd Division
**Brief History:** Founded 1884. Former Ground: John O'Gaunts Ground, moved to Sincil Bank in 1895. Founder-members 2nd Division Football League (1892). Relegated from 4th Division in 1987, promoted from GM Vauxhall Conference in 1988. Record attendance 23,196
**(Total) Current Capacity:** 11,100 (all seated)
**Visiting Supporters' Allocation:** 2,000 in Co-op Community Stand (part, remainder for Home fans)

**Club Colours:** Red and white striped shirts, black shorts
**Nearest Railway Station:** Lincoln Central
**Parking (Car):** City centre car parks; limited on-street parking
**Parking (Coach/Bus):** South Common
**Police Force and Tel No:** Lincolnshire (01522 529911)
**Disabled Visitors' Facilities:**
  **Wheelchairs:** The Simons and South (Mundy) Park stands
  **Blind:** No special facility
**Anticipated Development(s):** Following the replacement of the seats in the Stacey West Stand, Sincil Bank is once again an all-seater stadium.

**KEY**

**C** Club Offices
**S** Club Shop

⬆ North direction (approx)

❶ A46 High Street
❷ Sincil Bank
❸ Sausthorpe Street
❹ Cross Street
❺ Co-op Community Stand (away)
❻ A158 South Park Avenue
❼ Stacey West Stand
❽ Lincoln Central BR Station (½ mile)
❾ Family Stand

*Above:* 684973; *Right:* 684974

After the appalling season in 2001/02, the new campaign was one of some success for the Imps. Results on the last day ensured that Lincoln finished in sixth position, with both City and Bury edging Oxford United out of the frame, and thus a Semi-Final in the Play-Offs against local rivals Scunthorpe United. In the event City were to prove triumphant and thus faced Bournemouth in the Play-Off Final at Cardiff. Unfortunately, in a game that most fans will wish to forget, the match proved one too many for the squad as the Cherries romped home 5-2 thus ensuring that Lincoln will face another season in the Third Division. However, provided that the team can build on the late season form of 2002/03, there is every possibility that Keith Alexander's squad will again feature in the promotion campaign.

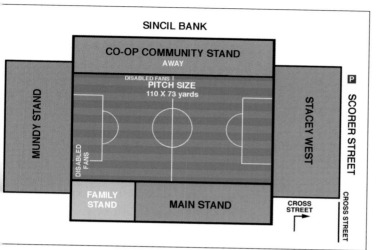

SINCIL BANK

CO-OP COMMUNITY STAND
AWAY

DISABLED FANS
PITCH SIZE
110 X 73 yards

MUNDY STAND

DISABLED FANS

STACEY WEST

P

SCORER STREET

FAMILY STAND

MAIN STAND

CROSS STREET

CROSS STREET

# LIVERPOOL

## Anfield Road, Liverpool, L4 0TH

**Tel No:** 0151 263 2361
**Advance Tickets Tel No:** 0870 220 2345
**Ticket Enquiries Fax:** 0151 261 1416
**Web Site:** www.liverpoolfc.tv
**Fax:** 0151 260 8813
**League:** F.A. Premier
**Brief History:** Founded 1892. Anfield Ground formerly Everton F.C. Ground. Joined Football League in 1893. Record attendance 61,905
**(Total) Current Capacity:** 45,100 (all seated)
**Visiting Supporters' Allocation:** 1,972 (all seated) in Anfield Road Stand
**Club Colours:** Red shirts, red shorts
**Nearest Railway Station:** Kirkdale
**Parking (Car):** Stanley car park
**Parking (Coach/Bus):** Priory Road and Pinehurst Avenue

**Police Force and Tel No:** Merseyside (0151 709 6010)
**Disabled Visitors' Facilities:**
  **Wheelchairs:** Kop and Main Stands
  **Blind:** Commentary available
**Anticipated Development(s):** After examining the possibility of expanding Anfield, the club has decided to explore the possibility of building a new 55,000 stadium costing £70 million on land about 200yd from Anfield adjacent to Stanley Park. If the project proceeds, after consultation with the council and local residents, it is hoped that the new ground will be open for the start of the 2005/06 season.

### KEY

**C** Club Offices
**S** Club Shop

↑ North direction (approx)

❶ Car Park
❷ Anfield Road
❸ A5089 Walton Breck Road
❹ Kemlyn Road
❺ Kirkdale BR Station (1 mile)
❻ Utting Avenue
❼ Stanley Park
❽ Spion Kop
❾ Anfield Road Stand

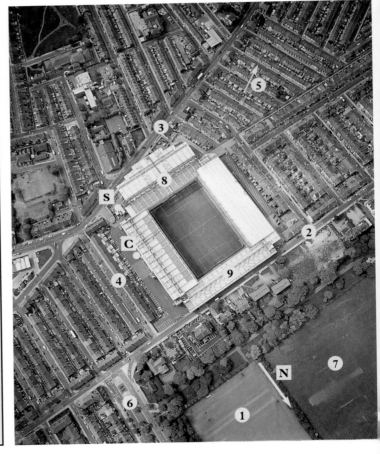

*Above:* 695700; *Right:* 695692

A curate's egg of a season for Gerard Houllier's team. A promising start to the campaign saw the team seriously considered as potential champions, followed by a dramatic loss of form that saw the club's worst run of league results for many years, completed by a late surge that saw the team make a late move towards a Champions League spot. In the end it all came down to a showdown with Chelsea at Stamford Bridge: if the home team avoided defeat, they would play in the Champions League but if Liverpool sneaked a win then the financial benefit would head to Merseyside. In the event, Chelsea won 2-1 ensuring that Liverpool would feature in the UEFA Cup. In other competitions, Liverpool again won the Worthington Cup, but failed to progress beyond the first phase of the Champions League, thereby entering the UEFA Cup, but were to defeated by Celtic over the two legs of the quarter finals. In the FA Cup, Liverpool suffered the indignity of a home defeat by Crystal Palace. In 2003/04, Liverpool should again challenge for honours, but without the income that the Champions League offers, it is hard to see Houllier being in a position to make major signings without having to offload players as well.

KEMLYN ROAD

CENTENARY STAND

PITCH SIZE
110 X 75 yards

ANFIELD ROAD

ANFIELD ROAD STAND

DISABLED FANS

AWAY

DISABLED FANS

KOP STAND

WALTON BRECK ROAD

DISABLED FANS

MAIN STAND

LOTHAIR ROAD

# LUTON TOWN

## Kenilworth Road Stadium, 1 Maple Road, Luton, LU4 8AW

**Tel No:** 01582 411622
**Advance Tickets Tel No:** 01582 416976
**Fax:** 01582 405070
**Web Site:** www.lutontown.co.uk
**E-Mail:** clubsec@lutontown.co.uk
**League:** 2nd Division
**Brief History:** Founded 1885 from an amalgamation of Wanderers F.C. and Excelsior F.C. Former Grounds: Dallow Lane & Dunstable Road, moved to Kenilworth Road in 1905. Record attendance 30,069
**(Total) Current Capacity:** 9,970 (all seated)
**Visiting Supporters' Allocation:** 2,200
**Club Colours:** Orange and blue shirts, blue shorts

**Nearest Railway Station:** Luton
**Parking (Car):** Street parking
**Parking (Coach/Bus):** Luton bus station
**Police Force and Tel No:** Bedfordshire (01582 401212)
**Disabled Visitors' Facilities:**
  **Wheelchairs:** Kenilworth Road and Main stands
  **Blind:** Commentary available
**Anticipated Development(s):** The club plans to relocate to a site close to the M1 but at present no timescale exists as to when this relocation will occur.

### KEY

- **C** Club Offices
- **S** Club Shop
- **E** Entrance(s) for visiting supporters
- **R** Refreshment bars for visiting supporters
- **T** Toilets for visiting supporters

↑ North direction (approx)

- ❶ To M1 Junction 11
- ❷ Wimborne Road
- ❸ Kenilworth Road
- ❹ Oak Road
- ❺ Dunstable Road
- ❻ Luton BR Station (1 mile)
- ❼ Ticket Office

*Above:* 695595; *Right:* 695588

hough most promoted teams struggle in their first campaign at a higher level, there are exceptions
Joe Kinnear's Hatters proved to be one of the latter. Although never seriously in the hunt for
omatic promotion or the Play-offs, finishing in ninth place, albeit 16 points off the Play-Off
itions, bodes well for the future. If Town can continue to progress, then the team should be aiming
nit the Play-Offs at the very least. However, immediately after the end of the season erstwhile
irman Mike Watson-Challis sold out to a mystery consortium and the first action of the new owners
to dismiss Kinnear and his assistant Mick Harford, much to the anger of fans. Following a bizarre
ing competition, in which Kinnear was one of the candidates, the club announced that Mike Newell
ld take over for the 2003/04 season.

# MACCLESFIELD TOWN

## Moss Rose Ground, London Road, Macclesfield, SK11 7SP

**Tel No:** 01625 264686
**Advance Tickets Tel No:** 01625 264686
**Fax:** 01625 264692
**Web Site:** http://www.mtfc.co.uk/
**E-Mail:** office@mtfc.co.uk
**League:** 3rd Division
**Brief History:** Founded 1874. Previous ground: Rostron Field moved to Moss Rose Ground in 1891. Winners of the Vauxhall Conference in 1994/95 and 1997/97. Admitted to Football League for 1997/98 season. Record attendance 10,041
**(Total) Current Capacity:** 6,307 (2,561 seated)
**Visiting Supporters' Allocation:** 1,900 (1,500 in Silkman Terrace; 400 seated in Estate Road Stand)
**Club Colours:** Royal blue, royal blue shorts
**Nearest Railway Station:** Macclesfield
**Parking (Car):** No parking at the ground and the nearest off-street car park is in the town centre (25min walk). There is some on-street parking in the vicinity, but this can get crowded.
**Parking (Coach/Bus):** As directed
**Police Force and Tel No:** Cheshire (01625 610000)
**Disabled Visitors' Facilities:**
   **Wheelchairs:** 45 places in Estate Road Stand
   **Blind:** No special facility
**Anticipated Development(s):** The new Estate Road (Alfred McAlpine) Stand, with its 1,497 seats, was completed towards the end of the season and officially opened on 5 May 2001. This is the first phase of a scheme to redevelop Moss Rose; the next phase will see a seated second tier raised above the existing terrace at the Silkman End. Other recent work has included the provision of permanent toilets at the away end.

---

### KEY

**C** Club Offices
**E** Entrance(s) for visiting supporters

⬆ North direction (approx)

❶ A523 London Road
❷ To Town Centre and BR station (1.5 miles)
❸ To Leek
❹ Moss Lane
❺ Star Lane
❻ Silkmans Public House (now closed)
❼ Star Lane End
❽ Silkman End (away section)
❾ Estate Road Stand

*Above: 688550; Right: 688570*

Another season of mid-table mediocrity saw the Silkmen under Dave Moss finish in 16th position some six points above the drop zone. One of a number of teams that flirted with the outer fringes of the relegation battle, Town could well face a much stronger challenge to retain its league status in the new season than last year.

# MANCHESTER CITY

## The City of Manchester Stadium, Sportcity, Manchester M11 3FF

**Tel No:** 0161 231 3200
**Advance Tickets Tel No:** 0161 231 2500
**Fax:** 0161 438 7999
**Web Site:** www.mcfc.co.uk
**E-mail:** mcfc@mcfc.co.uk
**League:** F.A. Premiership
**Brief History:** Founded 1880 at West Gorton, changed name to Ardwick (reformed 1887) and to Manchester City in 1894. Former grounds: Clowes Street, Kirkmanshulme Cricket Club, Donkey Common, Pink Bank Lane, Hyde Road and Maine Road (from 1923 until 2003). Moved to the City of Manchester Stadium for the start of the 2003/04 season. Founder-members 2nd Division (1892). Record attendance (at Maine Road) 84,569 (record for a Football League Ground)
**(Total) Current Capacity:** 48,000

**Visiting Supporters' Allocation:** tbc
**Club Colours:** Sky blue shirts, white shorts
**Nearest Railway Station:** Manchester Piccadilly
**Parking (Car):** As directed
**Parking (Coach/Bus):** As directed
**Police Force and Tel No:** Greater Manchester (0161 872 5050)
**Disabled Visitors' facilities:**
   **Wheelchairs:** tbc
   **Blind:** tbc
**Anticipated Development(s):** Following the completion of the City of Manchester Stadium after its use in the 2002 Commonwealth Games, Manchester City took over occupation for the start of the 2003/04 season. It would appear that, after several alternative proposals for reuse were examined, Maine Road will now be demolished.

---

**KEY**

⬆ North direction (approx)

❶ A662 Ashton New Road
❷ Commonwealth Boulevard
❸ Stadium Way
❹ A6010 Alan Turing Way
❺ North Stand
❻ South Stand
❼ West Stand
❽ East Stand
❾ National Squash Centre
❿ Warm-up track
● To Manchester city centre and Piccadilly station (1.5 miles)

*Above:* 695723; *Right:* 695776

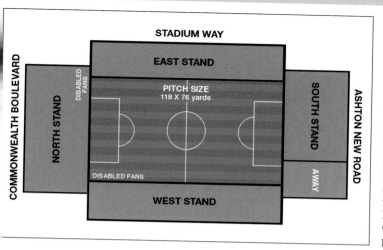

STADIUM WAY

EAST STAND

PITCH SIZE
118 X 76 yards

COMMONWEALTH BOULEVARD

DISABLED FANS

NORTH STAND

DISABLED FANS

SOUTH STAND

ASHTON NEW ROAD

AWAY

WEST STAND

For City's last season at Maine Road, Premiership survival was the order of the day and, unlike the team's last brief sojourn at this level, Kevin Keegan's squad achieved this aim with plenty to spare. Indeed, at one stage, it looked as though the team could sneak into the UEFA Cup. With Nicolas Anelka scoring a number of important goals and with the strike force supplemented by the mid-season capture of Robbie Fowler from Leeds, City were to finish in ninth place — a creditable effort for a promoted team, although the last game ever at Maine Road after 80 years was marred by the fact that Southampton won. With the new campaign and with the increased capacity offered by the City of Manchester Stadium, fans will be expecting further progress on the field and, perhaps, a serious challenge for a UEFA Cup spot.

# MANCHESTER UNITED

## Old Trafford, Sir Matt Busby Way, Manchester, M16 0RA

**Tel No:** 0161 868 8000
**Advance Tickets Tel No:** 0870 442 1999
**Fax:** 0161 868 8804
**Web Site:** www.manutd.com
**E-mail:** enquiries@manutd.co.uk
**League:** F.A. Premier
**Brief History:** Founded in 1878 as 'Newton Heath L&Y', later Newton Heath, changed to Manchester United in 1902. Former Grounds: North Road, Monsall & Bank Street, Clayton, moved to Old Trafford in 1910 (used Manchester City F.C. Ground 1941-49). Founder-members Second Division (1892). Record attendance 76,962
**(Total) Current Capacity:** 68,217 (all seated)
**Visiting Supporters' Allocation:** Approx. 3,000 in corner of South and East Stands

**Club Colours:** Red shirts, white shorts
**Nearest Railway Station:** At Ground
**Parking (Car):** Lancashire Cricket Ground and White City
**Parking (Coach/Bus):** As directed by Police
**Police Force and Tel No:** Greater Manchester (0161 872 5050)
**Disabled Visitors' Facilities:**
   **Wheelchairs:** South East Stand
   **Blind:** Commentary available
**Anticipated Development(s):** None at the present time.

---

**KEY**

**C** Club Offices
**S** Club Shop

↑ North direction (approx)

❶ To A5081 Trafford Park Road to M63 Junction 4 (5 miles)
❷ A56 Chester Road
❸ Manchester Ship Canal
❹ To Old Trafford Cricket Ground
❺ To Parking and Warwick Road BR Station
❻ Sir Matt Busby Way

*Above:* 688593; *Right:* 688583

Having finished 2001/02 without any additions to the Old Trafford trophy room and with a certain North London team regarding the footballing balance of power as having shifted irrevocably towards the Metropolis, 2002/03 was always going to be a season where the Red Devils sought to re-establish their pre-eminence. For much of the season, however, it looked as though Arsenal had established an unassailable lead in the Premiership, but as the season wore on, United found form at the right time and gradually overtook the Gunners to ensure that the title returned to Old Trafford. In the FA Cup, however, Arsenal retained its trophy, aided by a victory at Old Trafford, whilst in the Champions League, Real Madrid proved too strong over the two legs of the quarter final. With Sir Alex Ferguson, once destined for retirement but now clearly relishing the challenge again, still keen to add to the trophy collection the odds must favour United as being favourite to retain, yet again, the Premiership but the team will not have proved itself as one of the European greats until it has won the Champions League again.

# MANSFIELD TOWN

## Field Mill Stadium, Quarry Lane, Mansfield, Notts, NG18 5DA

**Tel No:** 0870 756 3160
**Advance Tickets Tel No:** 0870 756 3160
**Fax:** 01623 482495
**Web Site:** www.mansfieldtown.net
**E-mail:** mtfcstagshome@aol.com
**League:** 3rd Division
**Brief History:** Founded 1910 as Mansfield Wesleyans Boys Brigade, changed to Mansfield Town in 1914. Former Grounds: Pelham Street, Newgate Lane and The Prairie, moved to Field Mill in 1919. Record attendance 24,467
**(Total) Current Capacity:** 9,990 (all seated)
**Visiting Supporters' Allocation:** 1,800 (all seated) in South Stand
**Club Colours:** Amber with blue trim shirts, Blue shorts with amber trim

**Nearest Railway Station:** Mansfield
**Parking (Car):** Car park at Ground
**Parking (Coach/Bus):** Car park at Ground
**Police Force and Tel No:** Nottinghamshire (01623 420999)
**Disabled Visitors' Facilities:**
  **Wheelchairs:** Facilities provided in North, West and South (away) stands
  **Blind:** No special facility
**Anticipated Development(s):** Work on the Main Stand and on the North and Quarry Lane ends was completed in early 2001, leaving the Bishop Street Stand as the only unreconstructed part of Field Mill. Plans exist for this to be rebuilt but the time scale is unconfirmed.

### KEY

**E** Entrance(s) for visiting supporters

**R** Refreshment bars for visiting supporters

**T** Toilets for visiting supporters

⬆ North direction (approx)

❶ Car Park(s)
❷ Quarry Lane
❸ A60 Nottingham Road to M1 Junction 27
❹ Portland Street
❺ To A38 and M1 Junction 28
❻ To Town Centre
❼ Mansfield railway station
❽ North Stand
❾ Quarry Lane End (South Stand)
❿ Bishop Street Stand
● Main (West) Stand

*Above: 692632; Right: 692627*

predicated, following promotion at the end of the 2001/02 season, life for the Stags in the Second
Division was a struggle and, in early December, with the team rooted to the bottom of the Division,
Stuart Watkiss departed as manager. However, his replacement, Keith Curle, found life no easier and
the club was relegated back to the Third Division. With a number of ambitious teams vying for the three automatic promotion spots, Town may well struggle to achieve a quick return to the Second Division, but a spot in the Play-Offs should be achievable.

P

WEST STAND

PITCH SIZE
115 X 72 yards

QUARRY LANE
(SOUTH)
STAND
AWAY

NORTH
STAND

DISABLED
ENCLOSURE

BISHOP STREET
STAND

PORTLAND STREET

# MIDDLESBROUGH

## BT Cellnet Riverside Stadium, Middlesbrough, Cleveland TS3 6RS

**Tel No:** 01642 877700
**Advance Tickets Tel No:** 01642 877745
**Fax:** 01642 877840
**Web Site:** www.mfc.co.uk
**E-mail:** media.dept@mfc.co.uk
**League:** F.A. Premiership
**Brief History:** Founded 1876. Former Grounds: Archery Ground (Albert Park), Breckon Hill Road, Linthorpe Road, moved to Ayresome Park in 1903, and to current ground in Summer 1995. F.A. Amateur Cup winners 1894 and 1897 (joined Football League in 1899). Record attendance (Ayresome Park) 53,596, (Riverside Stadium) 34,800
**(Total) Current Capacity:** 35,100 (all seated)
**Visiting Supporters' Allocation:** 3,450 (in the South Stand)

**Club Colours:** Red shirts, red shorts
**Nearest Railway Station:** Middlesbrough
**Parking (Car):** All parking at stadium is for permit holders
**Parking (Coach/Bus):** As directed
**Police Force and Tel No:** Cleveland (01642 248184)
**Disabled Visitors' Facilities:**
  **Wheelchairs:** More than 170 places available for disabled fans
  **Blind:** Commentary available
**Anticipated Development(s):** There remain long term plans for the ground's capacity to be increased to 42,000 through the construction of extra tiers on the North, South and East stands, although there is no confirmed timetable for this work at the current time.

**KEY**

**C** Club Offices
**S** Club Shop

↑ North direction (approx)

❶ Cargo Fleet Road
❷ Middlesbrough station
❸ Middlesbrough town centre
❹ Middlesbrough Docks (1 mile) and Town Centre
❺ A66
❻ Borough Road
❼ Car Park
❽ South Stand

A slightly disappointing end to the season — four defeats in the final five games — took the shine off Steve McClaren's season at the Riverside Stadium. At one stage it looked as though Boro' could well have been vying for a place in the UEFA Cup but ultimately the team finished in 11th position, well outside the UEFA Cup places. It looks now as though Middlesbrough have a secure position in the Premiership: good enough not to get drawn into the relegation battle but never with enough strength to sustain a strong challenge for a top six position.

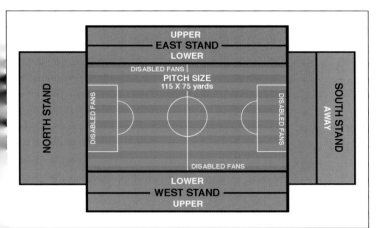

# MILLWALL

## New Den, Bolina Road, London, SE16 3LN

**Tel No:** 020 7232 1222
**Advance Tickets Tel No:** 020 7231 9999
**Fax:** 020 7231 3663
**Web Site:** www.millwallfc.co.uk
**E-mail:** webmaster@millwallplc.com
**League:** 1st Division
**Brief History:** Founded 1885 as Millwall
Rovers, changed name to Millwall Athletic
(1889) and Millwall (1925). Former Grounds:
Glengall Road, East Ferry Road (2 separate
Grounds), North Greenwich Ground and The
Den – Cold Blow Lane – moved to New Den
1993/94 season. Founder-members Third
Division (1920). Record attendance (at The
Den) 48,672 (at New Den) 20,093

**(Total) Current Capacity:** 20,150 (all seated)
**Visiting Supporters' Allocation:** 4,382 in
North Stand
**Club Colours:** Blue shirts, white shorts
**Nearest Railway Station:** South Bermondsey
or Surrey Docks (Tube)
**Parking (Car):** Juno Way car parking (8 mins
walk)
**Parking (Coach/Bus):** At Ground
**Police Force and Tel No:** Metropolitan (0207
679 9217)
**Disabled Visitors' Facilities:**
**Wheelchairs:** 200 spaces in West Stand
Lower Tier
**Blind:** Commentary available

**KEY**
**C** Club Offices
**S** Club Shop
**E** Entrance(s) for visiting
supporters

⬆ North direction (approx)

❶ Bolina Road
❷ South Bermondsey BR
❸ Surrey Quays Underground
❹ Zampa Road
❺ Ilderton Road
❻ To Rotherhithe New Road
and Rotherhithe Tunnel
❼ To New Cross
❽ Surrey Canal Road

lowing the success of Mark McGhee's team in its first season back in the First Division, in 2001/02, en they reached the Play-Offs, expectations at the New Den were high that the team would again ture in the race for the Premiership. In the event, however, the team initially struggled to replicate form of the previous season, although gradually reached the top half of the table. Ultimately, the ns finished in ninth place, eight points below the Play-Off positions (and with a considerably worse l difference). However, the team looks to have consolidated its position in the First Division and in must be considered strong contenders for the Play-Offs.

STOCKHOLM ROAD

BOLINA ROAD

WEST STAND
UPPER
LOWER

DISABLED FANS

PITCH SIZE
112 X 74 yards

UPPER
SOUTH STAND

LOWER

UPPER
NORTH STAND
AWAY
LOWER

LOWER
EAST STAND
UPPER

# NEWCASTLE UNITED

## St. James' Park, Newcastle-upon-Tyne, NE1 4ST

**Tel No:** 0191 201 8400
**Advance Tickets Tel No:** 0191 261 1571
**Fax:** 0191 201 8600
**Web Site:** www.nufc.co.uk
**E-mail:** admin@nufc.co.uk
**League:** F.A. Premier
**Brief History:** Founded in 1882 as Newcastle East End, changed to Newcastle United in 1892. Former Grounds: Chillingham Road, moved to St. James' Park (former home of defunct Newcastle West End) in 1892. Record attendance 68,386
**(Total) Current Capacity:** 52,193 (all seated)
**Visiting Supporters' Allocation:** 3,000 in North West Stand
**Club Colours:** Black and white striped shirts, black shorts

**Nearest Railway Station:** Newcastle Central
**Parking (Car):** Leazes car park and street parking
**Parking (Coach/Bus):** Leazes car park
**Police Force and Tel No:** Northumbria (0191 232 3451)
**Disabled Visitors' Facilities:**
  **Wheelchairs:** 103 spaces available
  **Blind:** Commentary available
**Anticipated Development(s):** With work now completed on both the enlarged Millburn and Sir John Hall stands, the capacity at St James' Park is now about 52,000. Further redevelopment at the ground is, however, problematic given the lie of the land on the north side, and the club has no immediate plans for further work once the current programme is completed.

**KEY**

**C** Club Offices
**S** Club Shop

⬆ North direction (approx)

❶ St. James's Park
❷ Strawberry Place
❸ Gallowgate
❹ Away Section
❺ To Newcastle Central BR Station (1/2 mile) & A6127(M)
❻ Car Park
❼ Barrack Road (A189)
❽ To A1 and North
❾ Corporation Street
❿ Percy Road
● Metro Station

*Above:* 694859; *Right:* 694852

Under the astute management of the 'Grand Old Man' of English football, Sir Bobby Robson, United were again well to the fore of challenging the top two for the title, although ultimately both Arsenal and Manchester United proved much stronger. The gulf between the top two and the rest was well illustrated by Manchester United's demolition of Newcastle at St James's Park, a result which went a long way to confirming the visitor's reclamation of the Premiership title. In the Champions League, Newcastle performed well in qualifying for the second group phase, although were unable to get into the knock-out stages. For 2003/04, having finished a creditable third in 2002/03, United are again in the Champions League and, with the experience gained, will again hope to make a decent challenge. In the Premiership, it is hard to see the title going other than to Man Utd or Arsenal, but Newcastle should again pose a potent threat. In terms of silverware, United's best hope may come in one of the cup competitions, although they can ill-afford to lose to lower division teams as they did to Wolves in the FA Cup in 2002/03.

# NORTHAMPTON TOWN

## Sixfields Stadium, Northampton, NN5 5QA

**Tel No:** 01604 757773
**Advance Tickets Tel No:** 01604 588338
**Fax:** 01604 751613
**E-Mail:** secretary@ntfc.tv
**Web Site:** www.ntfc.co.uk
**League:** 3rd Division
**Brief History:** Founded 1897. Former, County, Ground was part of Northamptonshire County Cricket Ground. Moved to Sixfields Stadium during early 1994/95 season. Record attendance 24,523 (at County Ground); 7,557 (at Sixfields)
**(Total) Current Capacity:** 7,653 (all seated)

**Visiting Supporters' Allocation:** 850 (in South Stand; can be increased to 1,150 if necessary)
**Club Colours:** Claret with white sleeved shirts, white shorts
**Nearest Railway Station:** Northampton Castle
**Parking (Car):** Adjacent to Ground
**Parking (Coach/Bus):** Adjacent to Ground
**Police Force and Tel No:** Northants (01604 700700)
**Disabled Visitors' Facilities:**
    **Wheelchairs:** Available on all four sides
    **Blind:** Available

### KEY

**C** Club Offices
**S** Club Shop
**E** Entrance(s) for visiting supporters
**R** Refreshment bars for visiting supporters
**T** Toilets for visiting supporters

↑ North direction (approx)

❶ South Stand (away)
❷ Athletics Stand
❸ To Upton Way roundabout (A45) with connections to Northampton Town Centre and M1 (North) and M1 (South)
❹ Car parks

*Above:* 688614; *Right:* 688605

Following a dismal run in the league, culminating in a 5-0 home defeat by Wycombe Wanderers, Kevan Broadhurst was sacked as manager on 6 January, the first managerial casualty of 2003. He was replaced the following day by Terry Fenwick, whose previous experience of management was a period at Portsmouth in the mid-1990s. Fenwick's reign was to last only seven matches as he was dismissed on 24 February with the team having dropped into the bottom four of the Second Division. Fenwick's replacement, in a caretaker role initially, was Martin Wilkinson; he was confirmed as full-time manager in early April. However, the new regime was unable to prevent the Cobblers dropping into the Third Division, with the team finishing last in the division having amassed only 39 points during the campaign.

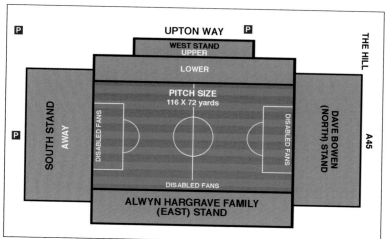

# NORWICH CITY

## Carrow Road, Norwich, NR1 1JE

**Tel No:** 01603 760760
**Advance Tickets Tel No:** 0870 444 1902
**Fax:** 01603 613886
**Web Site:** www.canaries.co.uk
**E-Mail:** reception@ncfc-canaries.co.uk
**League:** 1st Division
**Brief History:** Founded 1902. Former grounds:
   Newmarket Road and the Nest, Rosary Road; moved
   to Carrow Road in 1935. Founder-members 3rd
   Division (1920). Record attendance 43,984
**(Total) Current Capacity:** 16,000 (25,500 after
   completion of new South Stand and corner seats)
**Visiting Supporters' Allocation:** 300
**Club Colours:** Yellow with green side panel shirts,
   green shorts
**Nearest Railway Station:** Norwich
**Parking (Car):** City centre car parks
**Parking (Coach/Bus):** Lower Clarence Road
**Police Force and Tel No:** Norfolk (01603 768769)
**Disabled Visitors' Facilities:** tbc

**Wheelchairs:** tbc
**Blind:** Commentary available
**Anticipated Development(s):** Planning permission
   for the club's new £6.5million South Stand was
   granted in late April. The work will take Carrow
   Road's capacity to 25,500. As part of the
   redevelopment, permission was also granted for the
   construction of residential properties on part of the
   club's car park. The new stand will have a capacity of
   8,000 in a single tier but this can be increased later
   to 12,000 with the construction of a second tier. The
   work will also include a corner stand, for 1,500,
   between the South and River End stands. Work was
   due to start at the end of the season — after the cut-
   off date for photography — with an estimated
   completion date of early 2004. Whilst work is in
   progress, accommodation for away fans will be
   limited.

## KEY

**C** Club Offices
**S** Club Shop

↑ North direction (approx)

❶ Carrow Road
❷ A47 King Street
❸ River Wensum
❹ Riverside
❺ Car Park
❻ Norwich BR Station
❼ South Stand (prior to
   rebuilding)
❽ Geoffrey Watling (City)
   Stand
❾ Barclay End Stand
❿ The Norwich &
   Peterborough (River End)
   Stand

*Above:* 694297; *Right:* 694287

owing the disappointment of failure in the Play-Off final at the end of 2001/02, fans were no doubt
ecting Nigel Worthington's team again to make a sustained challenge either for automatic
motion or for the Play-Offs. In the event, however, the season was to end in disappointment with
team finishing in eight place, five points below the Play-Off zone and, even worse, separated from
zone by a resurgent Ipswich Town following the latter's poor start to the season. The Canaries will
again be one of the pre-season favourites for the Play-Offs at least and ought to be capable of achieving this.

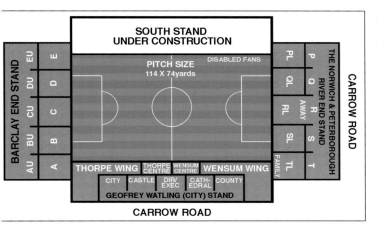

# NOTTINGHAM FOREST

## City Ground, Nottingham, NG2 5FJ

**Tel No:** 0115 982 4444
**Advance Tickets Tel No:** 0115 982 4445
**Fax:** 0115 982 4455
**Web Site:** http://www.nottinghamforest.co.uk
**E-Mail:** info@nottinghamforest.co.uk
**League:** 1st Division
**Brief History:** Founded 1865 as Forest Football Club, changed name to Nottingham Forest (c1879). Former Grounds: Forest Recreation Ground, Meadow Cricket Ground, Trent Bridge (Cricket Ground), Parkside, Gregory Ground and Town Ground, moved to City Ground in 1898. Founder-members of Second Division (1892). Record attendance 49,945
**(Total) Current Capacity:** 30,602 (all seated)
**Visiting Supporters' Allocation:** Approx 4,750

**Club Colours:** Red shirts, white shorts
**Nearest Railway Station:** Nottingham Midland
**Parking (Car):** East car park and street parking
**Parking (Coach/Bus):** East car park
**Police Force and Tel No:** Nottinghamshire (0115 948 1888)
**Disabled Visitors' Facilities:**
 **Wheelchairs:** Front of Brian Clough Stand
 **Blind:** No special facility
**Anticipated Development(s):** The club has long-term plans for the redevelopment of the Main Stand, with a view to increasing the ground's capacity to 40,000, but nothing will happen until the club reclaims a position in the Premiership.

---

### KEY

**C** Club Offices
**S** Club Shop
**E** Entrance(s) for visiting supporters

⬆ North direction (approx)

❶ Radcliffe Road
❷ Lady Bay Bridge Road
❸ Trent Bridge
❹ Trent Bridge Cricket Ground
❺ Notts County F.C.
❻ River Trent
❼ Nottingham Midland BR Station (1/2 mile)

*Above: 692575; Right: 692566*

though one of the teams in the First Division to have struggled financially for some years, under Paul
Hart the team has brought on a number of highly talented youngsters and, in 2002/03, this talent
began to find true expression on the football field. Whilst never strong enough to challenge for
automatic promotion, the team did succeed in reaching the Play-offs by finishing in sixth place.
However, defeat over the two legs in a fractious encounter with Sheffield United ensures that Forest
will again feature in the First Division in 2003/04. Provided that the club can (a) retain Paul Hart and
(b) continue to develop that talented squad, then there is every possibility that the new season should
again see Forest feature in the battle for promotion.

# NOTTS COUNTY

## Meadow Lane, Nottingham, NG2 3HJ

**Tel No:** 0115 952 9000
**Advance Tickets Tel No:** 0115 955 7210
**Fax:** 0115 955 3994
**Web Site:** www.nottscountyfc.co.uk
**E-Mail:** craig.mankelow@nottscountyfc.co.uk
**League:** 2nd Division
**Brief History:** Founded 1862 (oldest club in Football League) as Nottingham, changed to Notts County in c1882. Former Grounds: Notts Cricket Ground (Beeston), Castle Cricket Ground, Trent Bridge Cricket Ground, moved to Meadow Lane in 1910. Founder-members Football League (1888). Record attendance 47,310

**(Total) Current Capacity:** 20,300 (seated)
**Visiting Supporters' Allocation:** 5,438 (seated)
**Club Colours:** Black and white striped shirts, black shorts
**Nearest Railway Station:** Nottingham Midland
**Parking (Car):** Mainly street parking
**Parking (Coach/Bus):** Cattle market
**Police Force and Tel No:** Nottingham (0115 948 1888)
**Disabled Visitors' Facilities:**
  **Wheelchairs:** Meadow Lane/Jimmy Sirrel/Derek Pavis Stands
  **Blind:** No special facility

---

**KEY**

**E** Entrance(s) for visiting supporters

**R** Refreshment bars for visiting supporters

**T** Toilets for visiting supporters

↑ North direction (approx)

❶ A6011 Meadow Lane
❷ County Road
❸ A60 London Road
❹ River Trent
❺ Nottingham Midland BR Station (½ mile)
❻ Jimmy Sirrel Stand
❼ Kop Stand (away)
❽ Derek Pavis Stand
❾ Family (Meadow Lane) Stand

*Above:* 692577; *Right:* 692585

One of a number of clubs to descend into Administration during the course of the season, fans were probably increasingly concerned about events off the field rather than the team's mediocre performance on it. Whilst finishing in 15th position was a slight improvement on 2001/02, the club hovered just above the drop zone for much of the campaign and, whilst the club's future has now been secured, the inescapable conclusion is that the team will again struggle to retain its Second Division status.

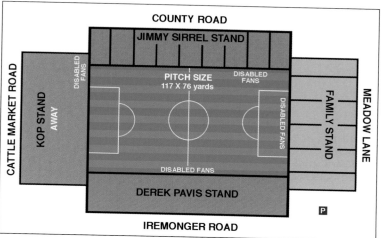

# OLDHAM ATHLETIC

## Boundary Park, Oldham, OL1 2PA

**Tel No:** 0870 7532000
**Advance Tickets Tel No:** 0870 7532000
**Fax:** 0161 627 5915
**Web Site:** www.oldhamathletic.co.uk
**E-Mail:** marketing@oldhamathletic.co.uk
**League:** 2nd Division
**Brief History:** Founded 1897 as Pine Villa, changed name to Oldham Athletic in 1899. Former Grounds: Berry's Field, Pine Mill, Athletic Ground (later named Boundary Park), Hudson Fold, moved to Boundary Park in 1906. Record attendance 47,671
**(Total) Current Capacity:** 13,624 (all seated)
**Visiting Supporters' Allocation:** 1,800 minimum, 4,600 maximum
**Club Colours:** Blue shirts, blue shorts
**Nearest Railway Station:** Oldham Werneth

**Parking (Car):** Lookers Stand car park
**Parking (Coach/Bus):** At Ground
**Police Force and Tel No:** Greater Manchester (0161 624 0444)
**Disabled Visitors' Facilities:**
  **Wheelchairs:** Rochdale Road and Seton Stands
  **Blind:** No special facility
**Anticipated Development(s):** The plans for the construction of a new 15,000-seat ground at Clayton Playing Fields in conjunction with the local RLFC club have been abandoned. As a result, Athletic will now seek to redevelop Boundary Park further, with the first phase being the construction of a new two-tier stand, costing £15 million, to replace the Lookers Stand. There is, however, no confirmed timetable for this work at the current time.

### KEY

**C** Club Offices
**E** Entrance(s) for visiting supporters

⬆ North direction (approx)

❶ A663 Broadway
❷ Furtherwood Road
❸ Chadderton Way
❹ To A627(M) and M62
❺ To Oldham Werneth BR Station (1½ miles)
❻ Car Park

*Above:* 685004; *Right:* 685008

Under new manager, Iain Dowie, who had been appointed in the summer of 2002, the Latics prospered in the Second Division and indeed achieved a notable cup upset when they defeated West Ham United at Upton Park in the Worthington Cup. In the league, a Play-Off position was secured, with the team finishing in fifth place only four points below promoted Crewe. However, facing QPR in the Play-Off semi-finals, the team came to grief, losing 2-1 on aggregate. The defeat ensures a further season of Second Division fare at Boundary Park in 2003/04, although the club could again feature in the hunt for automatic promotion. However, events in the close season have undermined preparations for the new campaign, and (a) the team has lost important team members and (b) is not guaranteed to exist by early August. Time will only tell if Oldham feature in the 2003/04 season.

# OXFORD UNITED

## Kassam Stadium, Grenoble Road, Blackbird Leys, Oxford OX4 4XP

**Tel No:** 01865 337500
**Advance Tickets Tel No:** 01865 337533
**Fax:** 01865 337555
**Web Site:** www.oufc.co.uk
**E-Mail:** admin@oufc.co.uk
**League:** 3rd Division
**Brief History:** Founded in 1893 as Headington (later Headington United)m changed name to Oxford United in 1960. Former grounds: Britannia Inn Field, Headington Quarry, Wooten's Field, Manor Ground and The Paddocks. The club moved back to the Manor Ground in 1925. Moved — finally — to new ground at Minchery Farm in 2001. Record attendance (at the Manor Ground) 22,730.
**(Total) Current Capacity:** 12,500
**Visiting Supporters' Allocation:** c5,000 in North Stand

**Club Colours:** Yellow with blue trim shirts and navy with yellow trim shorts
**Nearest Railway Station:** Oxford
**Parking (Car):** 1,100 spaces at ground
**Parking (Coach/Bus):** As directed
**Police Force and Tel No:** Thames Valley (01865 777501)
**Disabled Visitors' Facilities:**
  **Wheelchairs:** c80 disabled spaces
  **Blind:** No special facility
**Anticipated Development(s):** Although the club has plans for the construction of the fourth side of the ground there is no confirmed timescale as to when this work will be undertaken.

### KEY

**C** Club Offices
**E** Entrance(s) for visiting supporters

↑ North direction (approx)

❶ Grenoble Road
❷ To A4074
❸ Northfield School
❹ To Oxford city centre and railway station (four/five miles respectively)
❺ Blackbird Leys Estate
❻ Knights Road
❼ North Stand
❽ South Stand
❾ East Stand
❿ To B480

*Above:* 692183; *Right:* 692177

Following a disappointing season in 2001/02, when the club struggled in the Third Division, many considered that United would be one of the clubs facing the drop into the Conference. In the event, however, Ian Atkins' team defied these prophets of doom and were, until the final stages of the season, in with a real chance of making the Play-Offs. Unfortunately, events on the last day of the season, where United had to win and hope that Lincoln City lost, proved unfortunate; United achieved its part of the bargain with a 2-0 victory over York City, but the Imps achieved a 1-1 draw with Torquay thereby consigning Oxford to another season of Third Division football. Will it be third season lucky? Provided that the progress that was shown in 2002/03 is maintained, then the United faithful should be able to regard the forthcoming campaign with confidence.

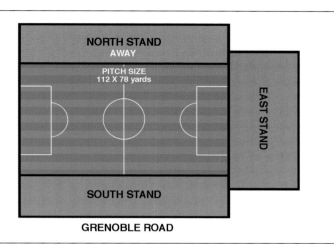

NORTH STAND
AWAY

PITCH SIZE
112 X 78 yards

EAST STAND

SOUTH STAND

GRENOBLE ROAD

# PETERBOROUGH UNITED

## London Road, Peterborough, Cambs, PE2 8AL

**Tel No:** 0870 550442
**Advance Tickets Tel No:** 0870 550442
**Fax:** 01733 344140
**Web Site:** www.theposh.com
**E-Mail:** info@pufc.theposhisp.com
**League:** 2nd Division
**Brief History:** Founded in 1934 (no connection with former 'Peterborough and Fletton United' FC). Elected to Football League in 1960. Record attendance 30,096
**(Total) Current Capacity:** 14,430 (7,669 seated)
**Visiting Supporters' Allocation:** 3,758 (756 seated)
**Club Colours:** Blue shirts, white shorts

**Nearest Railway Station:** Peterborough
**Parking (Car):** Peterborough
**Parking (Coach/Bus):** At ground
**Police Force and Tel No:** Cambridgeshire (01733 563232
**Disabled Visitors' Facilities:**
**Wheelchairs:** South Stand
**Blind:** No special facility
**Future Development(s):** Following the reroofing of the Moys and London Road ends, long term plans exist for the construction of a new Main Stand — for which plans have been prepared — and other work. However, there is no confirmed timetable for this at present.

### KEY

**C** Club Offices
**S** Club Shop
**E** Entrance(s) for visiting supporters
**R** Refreshment bars for visiting supporters
**T** Toilets for visiting supporters

↑ North direction (approx)

❶ A15 London Road
❷ Car Parks
❸ Peterborough BR Station (1 mile)
❹ Glebe Road
❺ A605
❻ To A1 (north) (5 miles)
❼ River Nene
❽ To Whittlesey
❾ To A1 (south) (5 miles)

*Above:* 685033; *Right:* 685030

A poor start to the season saw Barry Fry's Posh in the lower half of the Second Division, although, in a very tight division (only 10 points separated Posh in 11th place at the end from the relegation zone), a few extra points could make a dramatic difference to position. Under the experienced Fry, one of the longest serving managers in the Division, Peterborough should have the potential for a top half position in 2003/04.

GLEBE ROAD

THOMAS COOK SOUTH STAND
UPPER
DISABLED (D-WING)   LOWER
PITCH SIZE
112 X 71 yards

MOYS TERRACE (COVERED) AWAY

LONDON ROAD TERRACE (COVERED)

LONDON ROAD

ENCLOSURE   DISABLED

A STAND AWAY   MAIN STAND   WEST WING

# PLYMOUTH ARGYLE

## Home Park, Plymouth, PL2 3DQ

**Tel No:** 01752 562561
**Advance Tickets Tel No:** 01752 562561
**Fax:** 01752 606167
**Web-site:** www.pafc.co.uk
**E-mail:** argyle@pafc.co.uk
**League:** 3rd Division
**Brief History:** Founded 1886 as Argyle Athletic Club, changed name to Plymouth Argyle in 1903. Founder-members Third Division (1920). Record attendance 43,596
**(Total) Current Capacity:** 20,134 (15,684 seated)
**Visiting Supporters' Allocation:** 1,300 in Barn Park End Stand up to maximum of 2,000
**Club Colours:** White and green shirts, green shorts

**Nearest Railway Station:** Plymouth
**Parking (Car):** Car park adjacent
**Parking (Coach/Bus):** Central car park
**Police Force and Tel No:** Devon & Cornwall (0990 777444)
**Disabled Visitors' Facilities:**
  **Wheelchairs:** Devonport End
  **Blind:** Commentary available
**Anticipated Development(s):** Work on the three new stands at Home Park progressed well, with work being completed during the 2001/02 season. Plans, however, for the demolition of the existing Main Stand and its replacement have been deferred to September 2003 at the earliest as a result of the collapse of ITV Digital.

### KEY
**C** Club Offices
**S** Club Shop

↑ North direction (approx)

❶ Outland Road
❷ Car Park
❸ Devonport Road
❹ Central Park
❺ Town Centre & Plymouth BR Station (1/2 mile)

*Above:* 692218; *Right:* 692209

Following promotion at the end of 2001/02 season, Paul Sturrock's team again impressed in 2002/03 in pushing towards a Play-Off position. However, whilst the team ultimately finished in a creditable eighth place, this was 16 points below Cardiff City in sixth place and 15 below Tranmere Rovers in seventh and shows the gulf that existed between the top teams in the Second Division and the chasing pack. Not all was positive, however, during the season as, following a draw at Home Park in the 3rd round of the FA Cup, Argyle were defeated away by Conference team Dagenham & Redbridge. In terms of 2003/04, provided that the progress made on the field last year can be maintained, then Argyle should have the potential to make a much stronger push towards the Play-Offs at least.

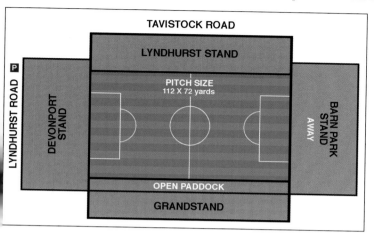

TAVISTOCK ROAD

LYNDHURST STAND

PITCH SIZE
112 X 72 yards

LYNDHURST ROAD

DEVONPORT STAND

BARN PARK STAND

AWAY

OPEN PADDOCK

GRANDSTAND

# PORTSMOUTH

## Fratton Park, 57 Frogmore Road, Portsmouth, Hants, PO4 8RA

**Tel No:** 02392 731204
**Advance Tickets Tel No:** 02392 618777
**Fax:** 02392 734129
**Web Site:** www.pompeyfc.co.uk
**E-Mail:** info@pompeyfc.co.uk
**League:** F.A. Premiership
**Brief History:** Founded 1898. Founder-members Third Division (1920). Record attendance 51,385
**(Total) Current Capacity:** 19,400 (all seated)
  **Visiting Supporters' Allocation:** 3,121 (max) in Milton Stand
**Club Colours:** Blue shirts, white shorts
**Nearest Railway Station:** Fratton
**Parking (Car):** Street parking
**Parking (Coach/Bus):** As directed by Police

**Police Force and Tel No:** Hampshire (02392 321111)
**Disabled Visitors' Facilities:**
  **Wheelchairs:** KJC Stand
  **Blind:** No special facility
**Anticipated Development(s):** It was announced at the end of the season that Pompey intended to redevelop the existing Fratton Park site. The work would involve the rotation of the pitch by 90 degrees in order to allow the construction of the new ground. It was intended that the new stadium, with an initial capacity of 28,000 (rising later to 36,000), would be completed by the start of the 2005/06 season at a cost of £26 million.

*KEY*

- **C** Club Offices
- **S** Club Shop
- **E** Entrance(s) for visiting supporters
- **R** Refreshment bars for visiting supporters
- **T** Toilets for visiting supporters

↑ North direction (approx)

- ❶ Alverstone Road
- ❷ Carisbrook Road
- ❸ A288 Milton Road
- ❹ A2030 Velder Avenue A27
- ❺ A2030 Goldsmith Avenue
- ❻ Fratton BR station (½ mile)
- ❼ KJC Stand

nder the astute management of Harry Redknapp, ably assisted by former boss Jim Smith, Pompey
ere in the top two virtually throughout the season and, despite the occasional hiccup (most notably a
ome reverse against relegation threatened Sheffield Wednesday), promotion to the Premiership was
hieved before Easter with the First Division title being secured towards the end of the season. With
s team combining youth and experience, Redknapp will be aware that the new season at the higher
vel will be one of challenge. With Pompey back in the top flight for the first time in 15 years, the
am will undoubtedly be one of the pre-season favourites for the drop. Whether this will happen
epends much on how the team is strengthened over the summer and on Redknapp's undoubted
ility to get the maximum from limited playing resources. Will 2003/04 see Pompey do a Birmingham
ity or a West Brom? Only time will tell, but the clever money will probably favour the latter.

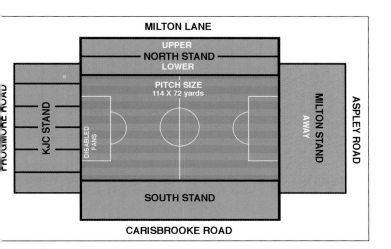

# PORT VALE

## Vale Park, Burslem, Stoke-on-Trent, ST6 1AW

**Tel No:** 01782 655800
**Advance Tickets Tel No:** 01782 811707
**Fax:** 01782 836875
**Web Site:** www.port-vale.co.uk
**E-Mail:** pvfc@port-vale.co.uk
**League:** 2nd Division
**Brief History:** Founded 1876 as Burslem Port Vale, changed name to 'Port Vale' in 1907 (reformed club). Former Grounds: The Meadows Longport, Moorland Road Athletic Ground, Cobridge Athletic Grounds, Recreation Ground Hanley, moved to Vale Park in 1950. Founder-members Second Division (1892). Record attendance 48,749
**(Total) Current Capacity:** 23,500 (all seated)
**Visiting Supporters' Allocation:** 4,550 (in Hamil Road [Phones4U] Stand)

**Club Colours:** White shirts, white shorts
**Nearest Railway Station:** Longport (two miles)
**Parking (Car):** Car park at Ground
**Parking (Coach/Bus):** Hamil Road car park
**Police Force and Tel No:** Staffordshire (01782 577114)
**Disabled Visitors' Facilities:**
**Wheelchairs:** 20 spaces in new Britannic Disabled Stand
**Blind:** Commentary available
**Anticipated Development(s):** Partial completion of the new 5,000-seat Lorne Street marks the end of current plans for the redevelopment of Vale Park.

### KEY

**E** Entrance(s) for visiting supporters

↑ North direction (approx)

❶ Car Parks
❷ Hamil Road
❸ Lorne Street
❹ To B5051 Moorland Road
❺ To Burslem Town Centre
❻ Railway Stand
❼ Sentinel Stand
❽ Hamil Road Stand
❾ Lorne Street Stand (under construction)
❿ Family Section

*Above: 691733; Right: 691738*

One of a number of clubs where events off the field overshadowed those on it, Port Vale under Brian Horton survived — just — in the Second Division, finishing in 17th position but only five points off the drop zone. Off the field, however, the very survival of the club was doubtful as the Valiants went into Administration in late 2002. At one stage it looked as though the Icelanders behind Stoke City were at the forefront of a plan to take Port Vale to the Britannia Stadium and thus to groundshare with Stoke City thus releasing Vale Park for redevelopment. In the event, however, a fan-based consortium, Valiant 2001, acquired ownership of the club from the Administrators towards the end of the season. With the club's immediate future now secured, Horton can look forward to the new season. However, it is hard to escape the conclusion that the Valiants will again struggle in the Second Division and relegation could be a serious possibility.

MAIN / RAILWAY STAND

FAMILY STAND AKA SENTINEL

PITCH SIZE
114 X 77 yards

HAMIL ROAD

HAMIL ROAD STAND

AWAY

BYCARS STAND

DISABLED FANS

P

LORNE STREET SIDE

BRITANNIA DISABLED STAND

LORNE STREET

# PRESTON NORTH END

## Deepdale, Sir Tom Finney Way, Preston, PR1 6RU

**Tel No:** 0870 442 1964
**Advance Tickets Tel No:** 0870 4421966
**Fax:** 01772 516213
**Web Site:** www.pnefc.net
**E-Mail:** enquiries@pne.com
**League:** 1st Division
**Brief History:** Founded 1867 as a Rugby Club, changed to soccer in 1881. Former ground: Moor Park, moved to (later named) Deepdale in 1875. Founder-members Football League (1888). Record attendance 42,684
**(Total) Current Capacity:** 22,225 (all seated)
**Visiting Supporters' Allocation:** 6,000 maximum in Bill Shankly Stand
**Club Colours:** White shirts, blue shorts
**Nearest Railway Station:** Preston (2 miles)
**Parking (Car):** West Stand car park

**Parking (Coach/Bus):** West Stand car park
**Police Force and Tel No:** Lancashire (01772 203203)
**Disabled Visitors' Facilities:**
**Wheelchairs:** Tom Finney Stand and Bill Shankly Stand
**Blind:** Earphones Commentary
**Anticipated Development(s):** The completion of the £3 million 6,100-seat Alan Kelly (Town End) Stand means that Deepdale has now been completely rebuilt on three sides. Planning permission has been granted for the construction for the construction of a new two-tier stand to replace the existing Pavilion Stand, taking the ground's capacity to 30,000. However, there is no confirmed timescale for the work at the present time.

*KEY*

**S** Club Shop

⬆ North direction (approx)

❶ A6033 Deepdale Road
❷ Lawthorpe Road
❸ Car Park
❹ A5085 Blackpool Road
❺ Preston BR Station (2 miles)
❻ Bill Shankly Stand
❼ Tom Finney Stand
❽ Town End Stand (under construction

*Above:* 692526; *Right:* 692522

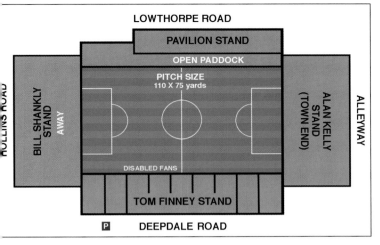

LOWTHORPE ROAD

PAVILION STAND

OPEN PADDOCK

PITCH SIZE
110 X 75 yards

ROLLINS ROAD

BILL SHANKLY STAND

AWAY

ALAN KELLY STAND
(TOWN END)

ALLEYWAY

DISABLED FANS

TOM FINNEY STAND

P DEEPDALE ROAD

A season of consolidation at Deepdale following the near miss of the Play-Offs at the end of 2001/02 and the appointment of ex-Scotland manager Craig Brown during the summer. Initially, it looked as though the Lilywhites were going to get dragged into the relegation battle as the season's early results looked less than encouraging, despite a triumph over Premiership outfit Birmingham City in the Worthington Cup. In the event, however, form and results improved and the club ended up in 12th position, well clear of the drop zone but still some 13 points below the Play-Offs. For the new season the Deepdale faithful will be expecting to see a serious challenge for the Play-Offs.

# QUEENS PARK RANGERS

## Loftus Road Stadium, South Africa Road, London, W12 7PA

**Tel No:** 020 8743 0262
**Advance Tickets Tel No:** 020 8740 2575
**Fax:** 020 8749 0994
**Web Site:** www.qpr.co.uk
**League:** 2nd Division
**Brief History:** Founded 1885 as 'St. Jude's Institute', amalgamated with Christchurch Rangers to become Queens Park Rangers in 1886. Football League record number of former Grounds and Ground moves (13 different venues, 17 changes), including White City Stadium (twice) final move to Loftus Road in 1963. Founder-members Third Division (1920). Record attendance (at Loftus Road) 35,353
**(Total) Current Capacity:** 19,148 (all seated)
**Visiting Supporters' Allocation:** 3,100 (maximum)

**Club Colours:** Blue and white hooped shirts, white shorts
**Nearest Railway Station:** Shepherds Bush and White City (both tube)
**Parking (Car):** White City NCP and street parking
**Parking (Coach/Bus):** White City NCP
**Police Force and Tel No:** Metropolitan (020 8741 6212)
**Disabled Visitors' Facilities:**
  **Wheelchairs:** Ellerslie Road Stand and West Paddock
  **Blind:** Ellerslie Road Stand
**Anticipated Development(s):** There is vague talk of possible relocation, but nothing has been confirmed. Given the constrained site occupied by Loftus Road, it will be difficult to increase the existing ground's capacity.

### KEY

**C** Club Offices
**S** Club Shop
**E** Entrance(s) for visiting supporters

↑ North direction (approx)

❶ South Africa Road
❷ To White City Tube Station, A219 Wood Lane and A40 Western Avenue
❸ A4020 Uxbridge Road
❹ To Shepherds Bush Tube Station
❺ To Acton Central Station
❻ BBC Television Centre
❼ Loftus Road
❽ Bloemfontein Road

134

*Above: 695957; Right: 695948*

aving failed, just, to make the Play-Offs at the end of 2001/02, optimism was high amongst the QPR ns that the team would go better in 2002/03 and, in this, they were not disappointed. Although the am failed to make one of the automatic promotion spots, by finishing in fourth place, three points elow promoted Crewe, QPR guaranteed themselves a place in the Play-Offs and, following victory over the two legs against Oldham Athletic, booked a place in the Play-off final against Cardiff at the Millennium Stadium. Despite dominating normal time, Rangers were ultimately to be defeated 1-0 after extra time, thus ensuring Second Division football again in 2003/04. However, provided that Ian Holloway can maintain his squad, there is every chance that QPR will feature in the hunt for automatic promotion in the new season.

# READING

## Madejski Stadium, Bennet Road, Reading, RG2 0FL

**Tel No:** 0118 968 1100
**Advance Tickets Tel No:** 0118 968 1000
**Fax:** 0118 968 1101
**Web Site:** www.readingfc.co.uk
**E-Mail:** comments@readingfc.co.uk
**League:** 1st Division
**Brief History:** Founded 1871. Amalgamated with Reading Hornets in 1877 and with Earley in 1889. Former Grounds: Reading Recreation Ground, Reading Cricket Ground, Coley Park, Caversham Cricket Cround and Elm Park (1895-1998); moved to the Madejski Stadium at the start of the 1998/99 season. Founder-members of the Third Division in 1920. Record attendance (at Elm Park) 33,042; (at Madejski Stadium) 22,034
**(Total) Current Capacity:** 25,000 (all seated)
**Visiting Supporters' Allocation:** 4,300 (maximum in the Fosters Lager South Stand)

**Club Colours:** White with blue hoops shirts, white shorts
**Nearest Railway Station:** Reading (2.5 miles)
**Parking (Car):** 1,800-space car park at the ground, 700 of these spaces are reserved
**Parking (Coach/Bus):** As directed
**Police Force and Tel No:** Thames Valley (0118 953 6000)
**Disabled Visitors' Facilities:**
  **Wheelchairs:** 128 designated spaces on all four sides of the ground
  **Blind:** 12 places for match day commentaries
**Anticipated Development(s):** The club has plans, if the need arises, to add an addition 5,000-seat section to the East Stand.

**KEY**
- **C** Club Offices
- **S** Club Shop

↑ North direction (approx)

- ❶ North Stand
- ❷ East Stand
- ❸ South Stand (away)
- ❹ West Stand
- ❺ Reading Stadium
- ❻ A33 Basingstoke Road
- ❼ To Reading town centre and station (two miles)
- ❽ M4 Junction (J11)
- ❾ Link Road to A33
- ❿ A33 southbound
- ● M4 westbound (towards Swindon)
- ⓬ M4 eastbound (towards London)

*Above: 688634; Right: 688627*

**P**

**WEST (ULTIMA BUSINESS SOLUTIONS) STAND**

**UPPER**

**LOWER**

**PITCH SIZE**
102 X 70 metres

SOUTH
(FOSTERS LAGER)
STAND

AWAY

NORTH
(NPOWER)
STAND

**EAST
(KYOCERA MITA)
STAND**

ACRE
ROAD

Although only promoted at the end of 2001/02 to the First Division, Alan Pardew's team proved the prophecies over the squad's potential to be correct as the team more than held its own in the First Division and achieved an impressive fourth place, thereby guaranteeing a spot in the Play-Offs. However, despite finishing above Wolves in the table, the Royals succumbed to the West Midlands' team over the two legs of the Play-Offs, s ensuring another season in the First Division for them. Fans will recall that the last time that ding almost made the top flight, the failure to do so resulted in an alarming collapse and ultimately gation to the Second Division. However, with the team's continued financial support, there is a ter likelihood of again challenging for promotion rather than fearing relegation.

# ROCHDALE

## Willbutts Lane, Spotland Stadium, Rochdale, OL11 5DS

**Tel No:** 01706 644648
**Advance Tickets Tel No:** 01706 644648
**Fax:** 01706 648466
**Web-site:** www.rochdaleafc.co.uk
**E-Mail:** office@rochdaleafc.co.uk
**League:** 3rd Division
**Brief History:** Founded 1907 from former Rochadale Town F.C. (founded 1900). Founder-members Third Division North (1921). Record attendance 24,231
**(Total) Current Capacity:** 10,262 (8,342 seated) following completion of Pearl Street Stand
**Visiting Supporters' Allocation:** 3,650 (seated) in Willbutts Lane (Per-Fit Windows) Stand

**Club Colours:** Blue shirts, blue shorts
**Nearest Railway Station:** Rochdale
**Parking (Car):** Rear of ground
**Parking (Coach/Bus):** Rear of ground
**Police Force and Tel No:** Greater Manchester (0161 872 5050)
**Disabled Visitors' Facilities:**
**Wheelchairs:** Main, WMG and Willbutts Lane stands – disabled area
**Blind:** Commentary available
**Anticipated Development(s):** None following completion of Willbutts Lane Stand.

---

### KEY
**C** Club Offices
**S** Club Shop
**E** Entrance(s) for visiting supporters

⬆ North direction (approx)

❶ Willbutts Lane
❷ A627 Edenfield Road
❸ Rochdale BR Station (¹/₂ mile)
❹ Sandy Lane
❺ To M62
❻ To M65 and North
❼ Pearl Street Stand
❽ Willbutts Lane Stand

*Above:* 687996; *Right:* 687986

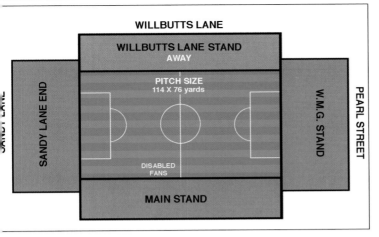

WILLBUTTS LANE

**WILLBUTTS LANE STAND**
AWAY

**PITCH SIZE**
114 X 76 yards

SANDY LANE END

W.M.G. STAND

PEARL STREET

DISABLED FANS

**MAIN STAND**

At the end of 2001/02 there was optimism at Spotland that, given the success of the team in reaching the Play-Offs, Rochdale would again mount a serious challenge for promotion. However, John Hollins, who had guided the team to the Play-Offs, departed at the end of the season and his replacement, as player-manager was Paul Simpson, for whom the post was his introduction to management. Under Simpson, Rochdale failed to maintain the progress of 2001/02 and finished the season in 19th position, only four points off the drop zone with the manager increasingly under fire from unhappy fans. After the season was over, the club moved quickly, with Simpson departing from the Spotland hot-seat to be replaced by experienced boss Alan Buckley.

# ROTHERHAM UNITED

## Millmoor Ground, Millmoor Lane, Rotherham, S60 1HR

**Tel No:** 01709 512434
**Advance Tickets Tel No:** 01709 309440
**Fax:** 01709 512762
**Web Site:** www.themillers.co.uk
**E-Mail:** shop@themillers.co.uk
**League:** 1st Division
**Brief History:** Founded 1877 (as Thornhill later Thornhill United), changed name to Rotherham County in 1905 and to Rotherham United in 1925 (amalgamated with Rotherham Town – Football League members 1893-97 – in 1925). Former Grounds include: Red House Ground and Clifton Lane Cricket Ground, moved to Millmoor in 1907. Record attendance 25,000
**(Total) Current Capacity:** 11,486 (6,949 seated)
**Visiting Supporters' Allocation:** 2,155 (all seated) in Railway End

**Club Colours:** Red shirts, white shorts
**Nearest Railway Station:** Rotherham Central
**Parking (Car):** Kimberworth and Main Street car parks, plus large car park adjacent to ground
**Parking (Coach/Bus):** As directed by Police
**Police Force and Tel No:** South Yorkshire (01709 371121)
**Disabled Visitors' Facilities:**
  **Wheelchairs:** Millmoor Lane
  **Blind:** Commentary available
**Anticipated Developments(s):** The club announced plans during the 2001/02 season for the rebuilding of Millmoor over a four-year period. The first phase of this work, for which there is no confirmed timescale, involves the construction of a new two-tier Main Stand costing some £4.25million.

---

### KEY
**C** Club Offices
**S** Club Shop
**E** Entrance(s) for visiting supporters
**R** Refreshment bars for visiting supporters
**T** Toilets for visiting supporters

↑ North direction (approx)

❶ Car Park
❷ To Rotherham Central BR Station
❸ A6109 Masborough Road
❹ Millmoor Lane
❺ To A6178 and M1 Junction 34

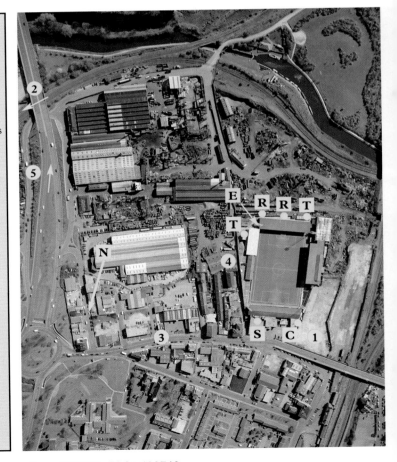

*Above:* 688743; *Right:* 688740

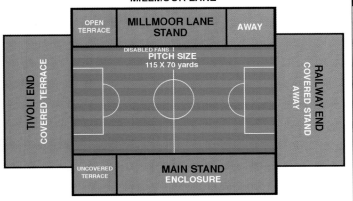

**MILLMOOR LANE**

| OPEN TERRACE | MILLMOOR LANE STAND | AWAY |
| --- | --- | --- |

DISABLED FANS
**PITCH SIZE**
115 X 70 yards

MASBROUGH STREET

TIVOLI END
COVERED TERRACE

RAILWAY END
COVERED STAND
AWAY

| UNCOVERED TERRACE | MAIN STAND ENCLOSURE |
| --- | --- |

The good news is that 2003/04 will see Premiership action at Millmoor; the bad news, for fans of the Millers, is that this will be in the form of the town's Rugby Union team rather than the football club. However, for the football club there was none of the end of season drama of 2001/02, where the team was almost relegated, and, in 2002/03 Ronnie Moore's team performed well and guaranteed themselves again First Division football by finishing in 15th position. With Sheffield Wednesday departing the Millers will be deprived of some local derbies in 2003/04 but should once again achieve a position of mid-table security.

# RUSHDEN & DIAMONDS

## Nene Park, Diamond Way, Irthlingborough, NN9 5QF

**Tel No:** 01933 652000
**Advance Tickets Tel No:** 01933 652936
**Fax:** 01933 650418
**Web Site:** www.thediamondsfc.com
**E-Mail:** dean.howells@airwair.co.uk
**League:** 2nd Division
**Brief History:** Rushden & Diamonds represents a merger between two teams — Rushden Town (founded in 1889) and Irthlingborough Diamonds (founded in 1946). The union, engineered by Max Griggs, occurred at the end of the 1991/92 season and from the start the club was based at the Nene Park ground of Irthlingborough Diamonds. Record attendance at Nene Park as a merged team 6,431
**(Total) Current Capacity:** 6,441 (4,641 seated)
**Visiting Supporters' Allocation:** 1,000 seats in the north side of the East (Air Wair) Stand

**Club Colours:** White with red and blue trim shirts; blue shorts
**Nearest Railway Station:** Wellingborough (six miles)
**Parking (Car):** 1,000 spaces at ground
**Parking (Coach/Bus):** As directed by the police
**Police Force and Tel No:** Northamptonshire (01933 440333)
**Disabled Visitors' Facilities:**
 **Wheelchairs:** 22 Places in the North Stand allocated to season ticket holders; 12 in the South Stand — limited number available on match by match basis
 **Blind:** No special facility
**Anticipated Development(s):** None

---

**KEY**

↑ North direction (approx)

❶ A6 Station Road

❷ To Rushden

❸ To Kettering

❹ Station Road (old)

❺ B5348 Station Road to Irthlingborough

❻ Diamond Way

❼ River Nene

*Above:* 688708; *Right:* 688704

Following the near miss at the end of the 2001/02 season, when the Diamonds lost in the Play-Off final against Cheltenham, 2002/03 was a season of considerable success for Brian Talbot's team, with promotion and the Third Division championship being gained in only the second season that the team had been in the Football League. The ironic thing about 2002/03 was that whilst the Diamonds were thriving in the Third Division, Cheltenham struggled in the Second and, indeed, the two teams will be swapping divisions in 2003/04. The feeling must be, however, that, with Diamonds' financial backing, the Northamptonshire outfit will be better placed to thrive at a higher level and it won't be a surprise to see the team well into the top half of the table.

DIAMONDS WAY

**NORTH STAND**

DISABLED FANS
**PITCH SIZE**
111 X 75 yards

DISABLED FANS

DISABLED FANS

WEST TERRACE

AWAY

AIR WAIR STAND

P

**SOUTH STAND**

# SCUNTHORPE UNITED

## Glanford Park, Doncaster Road, Scunthorpe DN15 8TD

**Tel No:** 01724 848077
**Advance Tickets Tel No:** 01724 848077
**Fax:** 01724 857986
**Web Site:** www.scunthorpe-united.co.uk
**E-mail:** scunthorpeunited@talk21.com
**League:** 3rd Division
**Brief History:** Founded 1899 as Scunthorpe United, amalgamated with North Lindsey to become 'Scunthorpe & Lindsey United' in 1912. Changed name to Scunthorpe United in 1956. Former Grounds: Crosby (Lindsey United) and Old Showground, moved to Glanford Park in 1988. Elected to Football League in 1950. Record attendance 8,775 (23,935 at Old Showground)
**(Total) Current Capacity:** 9,200 (6,400 seated)
**Visiting Supporters' Allocation:** 1,678 (all seated) in South (Caparo Merchant Bar) Stand

**Club Colours:** White shirts with claret and blue trim, white shorts
**Nearest Railway Station:** Scunthorpe
**Parking (Car):** At ground
**Parking (Coach/Bus):** At ground
**Police Force and Tel No:** Humberside (01724 282888)
**Disabled Visitors' Facilities:**
  **Wheelchairs:** County Chef Stand
  **Blind:** Commentary available
**Anticipated Development(s):** Although a new stadium – Glanford Park opened in 1988 – there is a possibility that, in the future, the existing Evening Telegraph Stand will be demolished and replaced by a two-tier structure.

### KEY

**C** Club Offices
**S** Club Shop
**E** Entrance(s) for visiting supporters
**R** Refreshment bars for visiting supporters
**T** Toilets for visiting supporters

⬆ North direction (approx)

❶ Car Park
❷ Evening Telegraph Stand
❸ A18 to Scunthorpe BR Station and Town Centre (1¹/₂ miles)
❹ M181 and M180 Junction 3

*Above: 688732; Right: 688726*

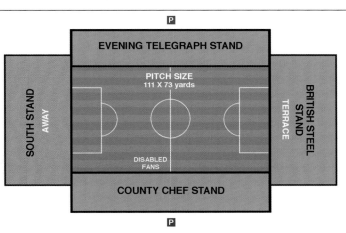

P

**EVENING TELEGRAPH STAND**

PITCH SIZE
111 X 73 yards

SOUTH STAND
AWAY

BRITISH STEEL
STAND
TERRACE

DISABLED
FANS

**COUNTY CHEF STAND**

P

Following the frustration of 2001/02, when Brian Laws' team came within an ace of making the Third Division Play-Offs, in 2002/03 the team went one better and finished in fifth place. This guaranteed a Play-Off semi-final against local rivals Lincoln City. Unfortunately, defeat both home and away in the Play-Offs means that United will again feature in the Third Division in 2003/04, but fans will undoubtedly expect to see — and may well do so — another serious push towards promotion.

# SHEFFIELD UNITED

## Bramall Lane, Sheffield, S2 4SU

**Tel No:** 0114 221 5757
**Advance Tickets Tel No:** 0114 221 1889
**Fax:** 0114 272 3030
**Web Site:** http://www.sufc.co.uk
**E-Mail:** info@sufc.co.uk
**League:** 1st Division
**Brief History:** Founded 1889. (Sheffield Wednesday occasionally used Bramall Lane c1880.) Founder-members 2nd Division (1892). Record attendance 68,287
**(Total) Current Capacity:** 30,936 (all seated)
**Visiting Supporters' Allocation:** 2,700 (seated) can be increased to 5,200 if needed
**Club Colours:** Red and white striped shirts, black shorts

**Nearest Railway Station:** Sheffield Midland
**Parking (Car):** Street parking
**Parking (Coach/Bus):** As directed by Police
**Police Force and Tel No:** South Yorkshire (0114 276 8522)
**Disabled Visitors' Facilities:**
  **Wheelchairs:** South Stand
  **Blind:** Commentary available
**Anticipated Development(s):** The club is contemplating construction of a corner stand, located between the Laver and Bramall stands, although there is no confirmed timescale for the work.

---

**KEY**
- **C** Club Offices
- **S** Club Shop
- **E** Entrance(s) for visiting supporters

↑ North direction (approx)

❶ A621 Bramall Lane
❷ Shoreham Street
❸ Car Park
❹ Sheffield Midland BR Station (¼ mile)
❺ John Street
❻ Spion Stand
❼ John Street Stand
❽ St Mary's Road

*Above:* 688043; *Right:* 688040

Although overshadowed in the league by Portsmouth and Leicester City, Neil Warnock's United can possibly claim to have been *the* team in the First Division, with semi-finals in both the Worthington Cup, where the team was unlucky to lose to Liverpool, and the FA Cup, where again the team was to be denied by, this time, Arsenal (and by one of the all-time great saves by David Seaman), alongside reaching the Play-Off final by defeating Nottingham Forest over the two legs. Finishing third in the table made the Blades the marginal favourites for the Cardiff match but a blistering first half saw Wolves take a 3-0 advantage that was to prove sufficient to consign United to defeat and thus another season of First Division football. Provided that the team suffers no loss of morale as a result of its nearly season, United will again be one of the favourites for promotion or the Play-Offs.

**JOHN STREET**

**JOHN STREET FAMILY STAND**

DISABLED FANS

BRAMALL LANE

BRAMALL LANE STAND

AWAY UPPER

LOWER

**PITCH SIZE**
113 X 72 yards

DISABLED FANS (TEMPORARY)

KOP STAND

SHOREHAM STREET

**LAVER (SOUTH) STAND**

**CHERRY STREET**

# SHEFFIELD WEDNESDAY

## Hillsborough, Sheffield, S6 1SW

**Tel No:** 0114 221 2121
**Advance Tickets Tel No:** 0114 221 2400
**Fax:** 0114 221 2122
**Web Site:** www.swfc.co.uk
**E-Mail:** enquiries@swfc.co.uk
**League:** 2nd Division
**Brief History:** Founded 1867 as The Wednesday F.C. (changed to Sheffield Wednesday c1930). Former Grounds: London Road, Wyrtle Road (Heeley), Sheaf House Ground, Encliffe & Olive Grove (Bramall Lane also used occasionally), moved to Hillsborough (then named 'Owlerton' in 1899). Founder-members Second Division (1892). Record attendance 72,841

**(Total) Current Capacity:** 39,859 (all seated)
**Visiting Supporters' Allocation:** 3,700 (all seated) in West Stand Upper
**Club Colours:** Blue and white striped shirts, black shorts
**Nearest Railway Station:** Sheffield (4 miles)
**Parking (Car):** Street Parking
**Parking (Coach/Bus):** Owlerton Stadium
**Police Force and Tel No:** South Yorkshire (0114 276 8522)
**Disabled Visitors' Facilities:**
    **Wheelchairs:** North and Lower West Stands
    **Blind:** Commentary available

### KEY

**C** Club Offices
**E** Entrance(s) for visiting supporters

↑ North direction (approx)

❶ Leppings Lane
❷ River Don
❸ A61 Penistone Road North
❹ Sheffield BR Station and City Centre (4 miles)
❺ Spion Kop
❻ To M1 (North)
❼ To M1 (South)
❽ West Stand

*Above: 688756; Right: 688754*

NORTH STAND

DISABLED FANS

PITCH SIZE
115 X 75 yards

LEPPINGS LANE

WEST STAND

UPPER TIER
AWAY

LOWER TIER

DISABLED FANS

SOUTH STAND

KOP STAND

PENISTONE ROAD

At the end of 2001/02, Wednesday managed to avoid the drop — just — but there were real fears that the new season would be a similar struggle against relegation to the Second Division. Unfortunately for fans of the team, these fears proved wholly justified as the team was in the bottom three for virtually the entire campaign. Inevitably, with a poor start to the season, manager Terry Yorath was soon to face the axe and in early November Chris Turner, from Third Division high-flyers Hartlepool, took over at Hillsborough. Despite the change of leadership there was little real progress on the field until towards the end of the campaign and, by then, it was probably too late. Ultimately, the team finished in 20th position, four points from safety, but fans will take heart from some of the end of season games, most notably the drubbing of Burnley, for the new season in the Second Division. As one of the relegated teams, Wednesday ought to have the pedigree to make a decent stab at automatic promotion, but much will depend on how much of the squad remains.

# SOUTHAMPTON

## The Friends Provident St Mary's Stadium, Britannia Road, Southampton SO14 5FP

**Tel No:** 0870 22 00 000
**Advance Tickets Tel No:** 0870 2200150
**Fax:** 02380 727727
**Web Site:** www.saintsfc.co.uk
**League:** F.A. Premier
**Brief History:** Founded 1885 as 'Southampton St. Mary's Young Men's Association (changed name to Southampton in 1897). Former Grounds: Northlands Road, Antelope Ground, County Ground, moved to The Dell in 1898 and to St Mary's Stadium in 2001. Founder members Third Division (1920). Record attendance (at The Dell) 31,044 (at St Mary's) 31,973
**(Total) Current Capacity:** 32,689 (all-seated)
**Visiting Supporters' Allocation:** c3,200 in North Stand

**Club Colours:** Red and white shirts, black shorts
**Nearest Railway Station:** Southampton Central
**Parking (Car):** Street parking or town centre car parks
**Parking (Coach/Bus):** As directed by the police
**Police Force and Tel No:** Hampshire (02380 335444)
**Disabled Visitors' Facilities:**
  **Wheelchairs:** c200 places
  **Blind:** Commentary available
**Anticipated Development(s):** Following completion of the new stadium the club has no further plans at present.

*KEY*

**C** Club Offices
**S** Club Shop
**E** Entrance(s) for visiting supporters

↑ North direction (approx)

❶ A3024 Northam Road
❷ B3028 Britannia Road
❸ River Itchen
❹ To M27 (five miles)
❺ To Southampton Central station and town centre
❻ Marine Parade
❼ To A3025 (and Itchen toll bridge)
❽ Belvedere Road
❾ North Stand

*Above:* 692503; *Right:* 692500

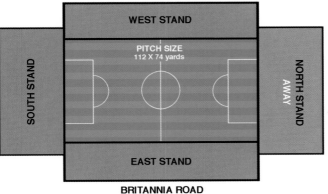

| WEST STAND | |
|---|---|
| | |

PITCH SIZE
112 X 74 yards

SOUTH STAND

NORTH STAND
AWAY

EAST STAND

BRITANNIA ROAD

A season of considerable progress on the field saw the Saints cement their position in the Premiership, finishing in an impressive eighth place, and also reach the FA Cup final for the first time since the team won the trophy in 1976. Unfortunately, a 1-0 defeat by Arsenal means that there is no addition to the trophy room, but Arsenal's already guaranteed place in the Champions League ensured that — win or lose — the Saints were in the UEFA Cup in 2003/04, thereby bringing European football to the new stadium for the first time. In Gordon Strachan, Saints have a committed and experienced manager well capable of bringing the best out of a team. Whilst it may be difficult to see the team reaching any of the cup finals in 2003/04, it is feasible to see the team continue to make progress in the league and challenge, perhaps, for one of the UEFA Cup spots.

# SOUTHEND UNITED

## Roots Hall Ground, Victoria Avenue, Southend-on-Sea, SS2 6NQ

**Tel No:** 01702 304050
**Advance Tickets Tel No:** 0870 174 2000
**Fax:** 01702 304124
**Web Site:** www.southendunited.co.uk
**E-mail:** info@southendunited.co.uk
**League:** 3rd Division
**Brief History:** Founded 1906. Former Grounds: Roots Hall, Kursaal, the Stadium Grainger Road, moved to Roots Hall (new Ground) 1955. Founder-members Third Division (1920). Record attendance 31,033
**(Total) Current Capacity:** 12,392 (all seated)
**Visiting Supporters' Allocation:** 2,700 (maximum) (all seated) in North Stand and North West Enclosure
**Club Colours:** Blue shirts, blue shorts

**Nearest Railway Station:** Prittlewell
**Parking (Car):** Street parking
**Parking (Coach/Bus):** Car park at Ground
**Police Force and Tel No:** Essex (01702 431212)
**Disabled Visitors' Facilities:**
  **Wheelchairs:** West Stand
  **Blind:** Commentary available
**Anticipated Development(s):** Although the club is still progressing with plans for the £12.5million 16,000 capacity stadium at Fossetts Farm, there is no timescale for this at present. In the meantime, the club has extended its lease at Roots Hall until 2006, so that it is likely that the team will be based here for at least the next three seasons.

---

### KEY

**C** Club Offices
**E** Entrance(s) for visiting supporters
**R** Refreshment bars for visiting supporters
**T** Toilets for visiting supporters

↑ North direction (approx)

❶ Director's Car Park
❷ Prittlewell BR Station (¹/₄ mile)
❸ A127 Victoria Aveneue
❹ Fairfax Drive
❺ Southend centre (¹/₂ mile)
❻ North Stand

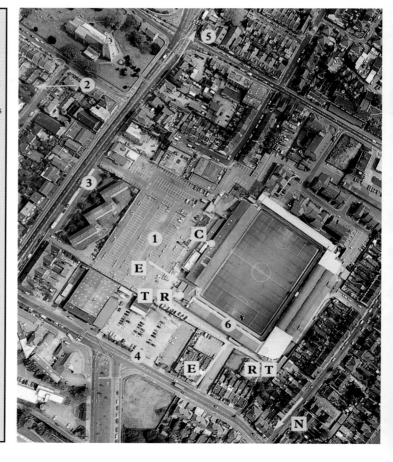

owards the end of March, ith the team hovering just pove the drop zone, anager Rob Newman and ssistant David Crown were cked. They were replaced itially by first team coach tewart Robson. Ultimately e new regime ensured hird Division survival rough finishing in 17th osition but it's hard to scape the conclusion that nother campaign against elegation beckons for the oots Hall faithful.

**SHAKESPEARE DRIVE**

**WEST STAND**

AWAY

ROOTS HALL AVENUE

FRANK WALTON STAND

UPPER TIER

LOWER TIER

DISABLED FANS

**PITCH SIZE**
110 X 74 yards

VISUALLY IMPAIRED

NORTH STAND

AWAY

FAIRFAX DRIVE

BLACK | GREEN | RED | YELLOW | BLUE

**EAST STAND**

**VICTORIA AVENUE**

# STOCKPORT COUNTY

## Edgeley Park, Hardcastle Road, Edgeley, Stockport, SK3 9DD

**Tel No:** 0161 286 8888
**Advance Tickets Tel No:** 0161 286 8888
**Fax:** 0161 286 8900
**Web Site:** www.stockportcounty.com
**E-Mail:** ftkcountrymarketing@email.com
**League:** 2nd Division
**Brief History:** Founded 1883 as Heaton Norris Rovers, changed name to Stockport County in 1890. Former Grounds: Heaton Norris Recreation Ground, Heaton Norris Wanderers Cricket Ground, Chorlton's Farm, Ash Inn Ground, Wilkes Field (Belmont Street) and Nursery Inn (Green Lane), moved to Edgeley Park in 1902. Record attendance 27,833
**(Total) Current Capacity:** 11,541 (all seated)
**Visiting Supporters' Allocation:** 800 (all seated) in Vernon Stand (can be increased by 1,300 all-seated on open Railway End if needed)
**Club Colours:** Blue with white stripe shirts, blue shorts

**Nearest Railway Station:** Stockport
**Parking (Car):** Street Parking
**Parking (Coach/Bus):** As directed by Police
**Police Force and Tel No:** Greater Manchester (0161 872 5050)
**Disabled Visitors' Facilities:**
  **Wheelchairs:** Main and Cheadle stands
  **Blind:** Headsets available
**Anticipated Development(s):** Although the club is still planning for the reconstruction of the Railway End, with the intention of constructing a new 5,500-seat capacity stand on the site, there is no time scale for this work (which had originally been planned for 1999/2000). Theoretically, the next phase after the Railway End would be an upgrade to the Vernon BS Stand, with the intention of making the ground's capacity 20,000.

### KEY

**C** Club Offices
**E** Entrance(s) for visiting supporters

↑ North direction (approx)

❶ Mercian Way
❷ Hardcastle Road
❸ Stockport BR station (1/4 mile)
❹ Railway End
❺ Main Stand
❻ Cheadle Stand
❼ Vernon BS Stand

*Above:* 695712; *Right:* 695706

**VERNON BS STAND**

AWAY

**PITCH SIZE**
111 X 71 yards

RAILWAY END
UNCOVERED TERRACE

CHEADLE STAND

DISABLED FANS

**MAIN STAND**

P **HARDCASTLE ROAD**

Following relegation at the end of 2001/02, County stuck with tyro manager Carlton Palmer as the team faced the new season in the Second Division. Unfortunately, County failed to make much of an impression at this level and ultimately finished in a mid-table position. Whilst never being threatened with the drop, the team also failed to make any sort of sustained challenge even for the Play-Offs. Repetition of such failure in 2003/04 could probably cost Palmer the managerial hot seat, but it is hard to escape the conclusion that this is perhaps the limit of County's ambitions at present.

# STOKE CITY

## Britannia Stadium, Stanley Matthews Way, Stoke-on-Trent ST4 4EG

**Tel No:** 01782 592222
**Advance Tickets Tel No:** 01782 592200
**Fax:** 01782 592201
**Web Site:** www.stokecityfc.com
**E-Mail:** info@stokecityfc.com
**League:** 1st Division
**Brief History:** Founded 1863 as Stoke F.C., amalgamated with Stoke Victoria in 1878, changed to Stoke City in 1925. Former Grounds: Sweetings Field, Victoria Ground (1878-1997), moved to new ground for start of 1997/98 season. Record attendance (at Victoria Ground): 51,380; at Britannia Stadium 27,109
**(Total) Current Capacity:** 28,383 (all-seater)
**Visiting Supporters' Allocation:** 4,800 (in the South Stand)
**Club Colours:** Red and white striped shirts, white shorts
**Nearest Railway Station:** Stoke-on-Trent

**Parking (Car):** The 650 parking spaces at the ground are for officials and guests only. The 1,600 spaces in the South car park are pre-booked only, with the majority held by season ticket holders. There is some on-street parking, but with a 10-15min walk.
**Parking (Coach/Bus):** As directed
**Police Force and Tel No:** Staffordshire (01782 744644)
**Disabled Visitors' Facilities:**
  **Wheelchairs:** 164 places for disabled spectators
  **Blind:** Commentaries available
**Anticipated Development(s):** There are long-term plans to increase the ground's to 30,000 by the construction of a corner stand between the John Smith Stand and the Boothen End but there is no timescale for this work.

---

**KEY**

↑ North direction (approx)

❶ Victoria Ground (site of)
❷ Stoke BR station
❸ A500 Queensway
❹ North Stand
❺ West Stand
❻ East Stand
❼ South Stand (away)
❽ A50 to Uttoxeter
❾ To M6 northbound
❿ To M6 southbound

espite having only been appointed in the summer, the ambitious Steve Cotterill departed the ritannia Stadium hot-seat on 11 October to become number two to Howard Wilkinson at inderland. In the immediate aftermath of his departure, Dave Kevan took over as caretaker. Initially looked as though George Burley, recently sacked by Ipswich, would take over; in the event he clined the offer and the board appointed Tony Pulis instead. The team battled hard to avoid the op, being in or just above the relegation zone for virtually the entire campaign. In the event, it was sults on the last day that ultimately determined City's fortunes. Brighton needed Stoke to lose whilst ining maximum points themselves in the away match at already relegated Grimsby. For Stoke fans, a 0 victory over high-flying Reading meant that the result at Blundell Park was irrelevant — it iaranteed First Division football again at the Britannia Stadium. Unfortunately, however, it is hard to cape the conclusion that 2003/04 will again be a battle to avoid the drop.

# SUNDERLAND

## Stadium of Light, Sunderland, SR5 1SU

**Tel No:** 0191 551 5000
**Advance Tickets Tel No:** 0191 551 5151
**Fax:** 0191 551 5123
**Web Site:** www.safc.com
**E-Mail:** communications@safc.com
**League:** 1st Division
**Brief History:** Founded 1879 as 'Sunderland & District Teachers Association', changed to 'Sunderland Association' in 1880 and shortly after to 'Sunderland'. Former Grounds: Blue House Field, Groves Field (Ashbrooke), Horatio Street, Abbs Field, Newcastle Road and Roker Park (1898-1997); moved to Stadium of Light for the start of the 1997/98 season. Record crowd (at Roker Park): 75,118; at Stadium of Light (48,353)
**(Total) Current Capacity:** 48,353 all-seater
**Visiting Supporters' Allocation:** 3,000 (South Stand)
**Club Colours:** Red and white striped shirts, black shorts

**Nearest Railway Station:** Stadium of Light (Tyne & Wear Metro
**Parking (Car):** Car park at ground reserved for season ticket holders. Limited on-street parking (but the police may decide to introduce restrictions). Otherwise off-street parking in city centre
**Parking (Coach/Bus):** As directed
**Police Force and Tel No:** Tyne & Wear (0191 510 2020)
**Disabled Visitors' Facilities:**
  **Wheelchairs:** 180 spots
  **Blind:** Commentary available
**Anticipated Development(s):** Work on the £6 million expansion of the North Stand at the Stadium of Light was completed during 2000/01, taking the ground's capacity to over 48,000. This is the first phase of a three-phase scheme to increase the ground's capacity to 66,000.

### KEY

**C** Club Offices
**S** Club Shop
**E** Entrance(s) for visiting supporters

↑ North direction (approx)

❶ River Wear
❷ North (Vaux) Stand
❸ South (Metro FM) Stand (away)
❹ To Sunderland BR station (0.5 mile)
❺ Southwick Road
❻ Stadium Way
❼ Millennium Way
❽ Hay Street
❾ To Wearmouth Bridge (via A1018 North Bridge Street) to City Centre

*Above: 688659; Right: 688650*

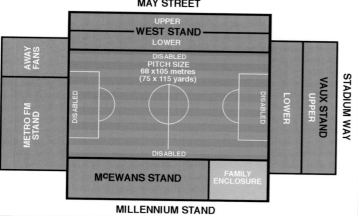

**MAY STREET**

UPPER
**WEST STAND**
LOWER

AWAY FANS

DISABLED
PITCH SIZE
68 x 105 metres
(75 x 115 yards)

METRO FM STAND

DISABLED

DISABLED

DISABLED

LOWER

VAUX STAND

UPPER

STADIUM WAY

**McEWANS STAND**

FAMILY ENCLOSURE

**MILLENNIUM STAND**

After holding the Sunderland job for more than seven years, Peter Reid's tenure at the Stadium of Light ended in early October. Despite the high-profile signings of Tore Andre Flo and Marcus Stewart, the team had again performed poorly in the Premiership, and Reid's position became increasingly untenable. He was quickly replaced by Howard Wilkinson, with ex-Stoke boss Steve Cotterill joining as assistant. However, it was a relationship doomed to failure and, on 10 March, with the Black Cats rooted to bottom spot having won two of the 20 league games since the duo was appointed, Wilkinson and Cotterill departed. A couple of days later ex-Ireland boss Mick McCarthy was unveiled, not unexpectedly, as the team's new boss. McCarthy's reign in the Premiership was even more disastrous with the team achieving the unenviable record of losing every game. McCarthy remains in the role but Sunderland, like all relegated teams, face a struggle both on and off the field in the new season.

# SWANSEA CITY

## Vetch Field, Swansea SA1 3SU

**Tel No:** 01792 633400
**Advance Tickets Tel No:** 01792 633425
**Fax:** 01792 646120
**Web Site:** www.swanseacity.net
**E-mail:** info@swansafc.freeserve.co.uk
**League:** 3rd Division
**Brief History:** Founded 1900 as Swansea Town, changed to Swansea City in 1970. Former Grounds: various, including Recreation Ground. Moved to Vetch Field in 1912. Founder-members Third Division (1920). Record attendance 32,796
**(Total) Current Capacity:** 13,500 (3,414 seated)
**Visiting Supporters' Allocation:** 1,541 (on the West Terrace)
**Club Colours:** White shirts, white shorts
**Nearest Railway Station:** Swansea High Street
**Parking (Car):** Kingsway car park and adjacent Clarence Terrace (supervised car park)

**Parking (Coach/Bus):** As directed by Police
**Police Force and Tel No:** South Wales (01792 456999)
**Disabled Visitors' Facilities:**
  **Wheelchairs:** Glamorgan Street
  **Blind:** No special facility
**Anticipated Development(s):** Plans for the conversion of the Morfa Stadium, currently used for athletics, into a 20,000 all-seater stadium are progressing now that planning permission has been granted, although there is no confirmed timescale at present. The new ground will be largely funded by Swansea City Council and will provide a home for both City and the town's rugby club. In the short term, the close season will see work undertaken at the Vetch, which will result in an increased capacity of 13,500 for the new season.

### KEY

**C** Club Offices
**S** Club Shop
**E** Entrance(s) for visiting supporters
**R** Refreshment bars for visiting supporters
**T** Toilets for visiting supporters

↑ North direction (approx)

❶ Glamorgan Street
❷ William Street
❸ Richardson Street
❹ A4067 Oystermouth Road (8 miles to M4 Junction 42)
❺ Swansea High Street BR Station (½ mile)
❻ Supervised Car Park
❼ North Bank

*Above:* 615398; *Right:* 615403

With the club not having won a game since 11 September and with the team bottom of the Third Division, Nick Cusack resigned as player-manager on 31 October. He was replaced by experienced manager Brian Flynn. Under Flynn, the team continued to struggle and were serious candidates for the drop into the Conference at one stage. In the event, however, the Swans finished in 22nd position, one point above the drop zone. Preserving the team's League status in 2002/03 was all important, but fans will be expecting much more in 2003/04 — particularly as City is now the only Welsh team in the Nationwide League's basement division.

MADOC STREET

NORTH BANK
COVERED TERRACE

OPEN PADDOCK

PITCH SIZE
112 X 74 yards

RICHARDSON STREET

WEST TERRACE
PART COVERED TERRACE
AWAY

DISABLED
FANS

CENTRE STAND
JEWSON STAND

EAST TERRACE
COVERED

EAST STAND

WILLIAM STREET

GLAMORGAN STREET

# SWINDON TOWN

## County Ground, County Road, Swindon, SN1 2ED

**Tel No:** 01793 333700
**Advance Tickets Tel No:** 01793 333777
**Fax:** 01793 333703
**Web Site:** www.swindontownfc.co.uk
**E-Mail:** stfc_enquiries@hotmail.com
**League:** 2nd Division
**Brief History:** Founded 1881. Former Grounds: Quarry Ground, Globe Road, Croft Ground, County Ground (adjacent to current Ground and now Cricket Ground), moved to current County Ground in 1896. Founder-members Third Division (1920). Record attendance 32,000
**(Total) Current Capacity:** 15,700 (all seated)
**Visiting Supporters' Allocation:** 3,342 (all seated) in Arkell's Stand and Stratton Bank (open)

**Club Colours:** Red shirts, white shorts
**Nearest Railway Station:** Swindon
**Parking (Car):** Town Centre
**Parking (Coach/Bus):** Adjacent car park
**Police Force and Tel No:** Wiltshire (01793 528111)
**Disabled Visitors' Facilities:**
  **Wheelchairs:** In front of Arkell's Stand
  **Blind:** Commentary available
**Anticipated Development(s):** Outline planning permission has been granted for the construction of a new £35 million stadium adjacent to the M4. The new stadium, which will provide seating for 25,000, was scheduled for completion by mid-2003 but has not been progressed at this stage.

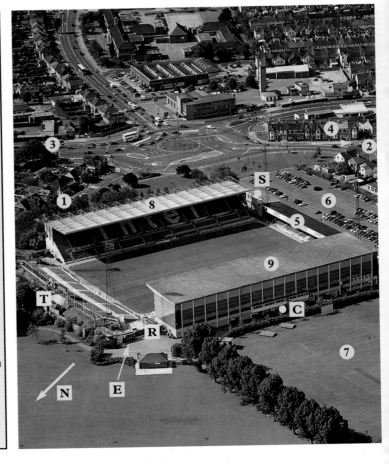

**KEY**

**C** Club Offices
**S** Club Shop
**E** Entrance(s) for visiting supporters
**R** Refreshment bars for visiting supporters
**T** Toilets for visiting supporters

↑ North direction (approx)

❶ Shrivenham Road
❷ County Ground
❸ A345 Queens Drive (M4 Junction 15 – 3½ miles)
❹ Swindon BR Station (½ mile)
❺ Town End
❻ Car Park
❼ County Cricket Ground
❽ Nationwide Stand
❾ Arkell's Stand

**ARKELLS STAND**

| AR1 | FAM | AR3 | AR4 | |
|-----|-----|-----|-----|-----|
| KIDS | AR2 | ENCLOSURE | | AWAY |

DISABLED FANS

**PITCH SIZE**
**114 X 74 yards**

COUNTY ROAD

**TOWN END**
(OVERFLOW)

**STRATTON BANK STAND**
(OPEN STAND)
AWAY

DISABLED FANS

**ENCLOSURE**

| NW6 | NW5 | NW4 | NW3 | NW2 | NW1 |
|-----|-----|-----|-----|-----|-----|
| | | **SOUTH STAND** | | | |

**SHRIVENHAM ROAD**

A season of some promise at the County ground saw Andy King's team improve over its performance in 2001/02 and reach the dizzy heights of 10th in the Second Division. Never strong enough for the push towards promotion or weak enough to be sucked into the relegation battle, the team achieved security and a further campaign in the Second Division. However, it is hard to see Town achieving much more than a similar position in 2003/04 considering that the team finished more than 20 points off the Play-Off zone in 2002/03.

# TORQUAY UNITED

## Plainmoor Ground, Torquay, TQ1 3PS

**Tel No:** 01803 328666
**Advance Tickets Tel No:** 01803 328666
**Fax:** 01803 323976
**Web Site:** www.torquayunited.com
**E-Mail:** gullsfc@freeuk.com
**League:** 3rd Division
**Brief History:** Founded 1898, as Torquay United, amalgamated with Ellacombe in 1910, changed name to Torquay Town. Amalgamated with Babbacombe in 1921, changed name to Torquay United. Former Grounds: Teignmouth Road, Torquay Recreation Ground, Cricketfield Road & Torquay Cricket Ground, moved to Plainmoor (Ellacombe Ground) in 1910. Record attendance 21,908
**(Total) Current Capacity:** 6,283 (2,446 seated)
**Visiting Supporters' Allocation:** 1,004 (196 seated)

**Club Colours:** Yellow with white stripe shirts, yellow shorts
**Nearest Railway Station:** Torquay (2 miles)
**Parking (Car):** Street parking
**Parking (Coach/Bus):** Lymington Road coach station
**Police Force and Tel No:** Devon & Cornwall (01803 214491)
**Disabled Visitors' Facilities:**
  **Wheelchairs:** Ellacombe End
  **Blind:** Commentary available
**Anticipated Development(s):** There are proposals for a joint project with a local school for the rebuilding of the Main Stand. This would give United a 2,500-seat stand but there is no confirmed timescale.

### KEY
**C** Club Offices
**S** Club Shop
**E** Entrance(s) for visiting supporters
**R** Refreshment bars for visiting supporters
**T** Toilets for visiting supporters

↑ North direction (approx)

❶ Warbro Road
❷ B3202 Marychurch Road
❸ Marnham Road
❹ Torquay BR Station (2 miles)
❺ To A38
❻ Babbacombe End

*Above: 692266; Right: 692257*

A season of reasonable promise on the south coast saw Torquay United under Leroy Rosenior achieve a creditable ninth in the Third Division, being in the hunt for a Play-Off spot for much of the season. Provided that the team can maintain the momentum, then there must be every likelihood of the team again making a serious push towards the Play-Offs. For fans of the team, the new season will be slightly strange as, for the first time in many years, there will be no local Derbies as Plymouth remain in the Second Division and Exeter City were relegated to the Conference.

**HOMELANDS LANE**

AWAY | **MAIN STAND**

WARBRO ROAD

WARBRO ROAD
COVERED TERRACE
AWAY

PITCH SIZE
112 X 74 yards

DISABLED FANS

HERALD EXPRESS
FAMILY STAND

ELLACOMBE ROAD

**CARLSBERG POPULAR TERRACE**

**MARNHAM ROAD**

# TOTTENHAM HOTSPUR

## Bill Nicholson Way, 748 High Street, Tottenham, London N17 0AP

**Tel No:** 0208 365 5000
**Ticket Line:** 08700 112222
**Fax:** 020 8365 5005
**Web Site:** www.spurs.co.uk
**E-Mail:** mail@spurs.co.uk
**League:** F.A. Premier
**Brief History:** Founded 1882 as 'Hotspur', changed name to Tottenham Hotspur in 1885. Former Grounds: Tottenham Marshes and Northumberland Park, moved to White Hart Lane in 1899. F.A. Cup winner 1901 (as a non-League club). Record attendance 75,038
**(Total) Current Capacity:** 36,257 (all seated)
**Visiting Supporters' Allocation:** 3,000 (in South Stands)
**Club Colours:** White shirts, navy blue shorts
**Nearest Railway Station:** White Hart Lane plus Seven Sisters and Manor House (tube)

**Parking (Car):** Street parking (min ¼ mile from ground)
**Parking (Coach/Bus):** Northumberland Park coach park
**Police Force and Tel No:** Metropolitan (0208 801 3443)
**Disabled Visitors' Facilities:**
   **Wheelchairs:** North and South Stands (by prior arrangement)
   **Blind:** Commentary available
**Anticipated Development(s):** The local council gave permission in October 2001 for the construction of a third tier on the East Stand taking capacity to 44,000, although there is no schedule for the work and it depends on other local regeneration work. Despite the potential that this increase offers, the club is still interested ultimately in relocation.

### KEY

**C** Club Offices
**S** Club Shop
**E** Entrance(s) for visiting supporters
**R** Refreshment bars for visiting supporters
**T** Toilets for visiting supporters

↑ North direction (approx)

❶ Park Lane
❷ A1010 High Road
❸ White Hart Lane BR station
❹ Paxton Road
❺ Worcester Avenue
❻ West Stand
❼ South Stand

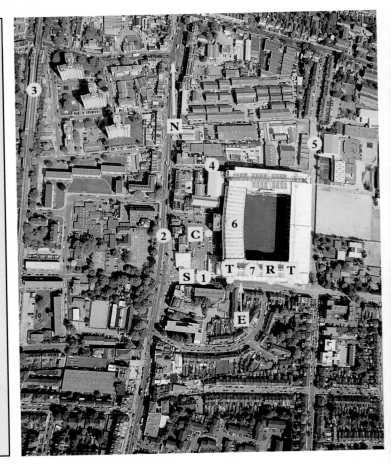

*Above:* 695627; *Right:* 695621

This was supposed to be the season that Glenn Hoddle led Spurs back towards the promised land (Ok, at least a place in the UEFA Cup). In the event, the White Hart Lane faithful had to witness yet another season of being overshadowed by their North London rivals and, by the end of the campaign, there were distinct whispers about Hoddle's abilities. Ultimately, Spurs ended the season in 10th position, 10 points below the UEFA Cup spot and failed to make much of an impact in either Cup competition. With one or two prominent players, such as Teddy Sheringham, on the way out, the early part of the 2003/04 campaign could be make or break for Hoddle; a good start could see the fans get behind him again but an indifferent one could see the whispers develop into a fully fledged 'Hoddle Out' campaign. Could the ex-England boss be the first managerial casualty in the Premiership in 2003/04 — on form shown towards the end of 2002/03, it could well be a very serious possibility.

# TRANMERE ROVERS

## Prenton Park, Prenton Road West, Birkenhead, CH42 9PY

**Tel No:** 0151 609 3333
**Advance Tickets Tel No:** 0151 609 3322
**Fax:** 0151 609 0606
**Web Site:** http://www.tranmererovers.co.uk
**League:** 2nd Division
**Brief History:** Founded 1884 as Belmont F.C., changed name to Tranmere Rovers in 1885 (not connected to earlier 'Tranmere Rovers'). Former grounds: Steele's Field and Ravenshaw's Field (also known as Old Prenton Park, ground of Tranmere Rugby Club), moved to (new) Prenton Park in 1911. Founder-members 3rd Division North (1921). Record attendance 24,424

**(Total) Current Capacity:** 16,587 (all seated)
**Visiting Supporters' Allocation:** 2,500 (all-seated) in Cow Shed Stand
**Club Colours:** White shirts, white shorts
**Nearest Railway Station:** Hamilton Square or Rock Ferry
**Parking (Car):** Car park at Ground
**Parking (Coach/Bus):** Car park at Ground
**Police Force and Tel No:** Merseyside (0151 709 6010)
**Disabled Visitors' Facilities:**
**Wheelchairs:** Main Stand
**Blind:** Commentary available

---

## KEY

**C** Club Offices
**S** Club Shop
**E** Entrance(s) for visiting supporters

↑ North direction (approx)

❶ Car Park
❷ Prenton Road West
❸ Borough Road
❹ M53 Junction 4 (B5151) – 3 miles
❺ Birkenhead (1 mile)
❻ Cow Shed Stand
❼ Kop Shed

*Above:* 692608; *Right:* 692605

Under Ray Mathias, Rovers showed significant promise in 2002/03 and just failed to reach the Play-Offs, being pipped to the all-important sixth spot by Cardiff City by a single point (although City did have a significantly better goal difference). Provided that the team's momentum can be maintained, there is every possibility that the team can again make a serious push towards promotion and regain its First Division status.

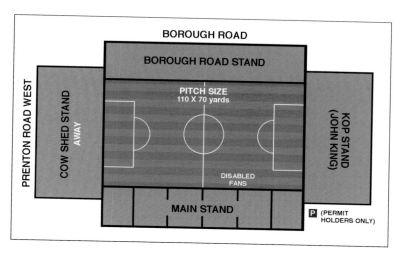

BOROUGH ROAD

BOROUGH ROAD STAND

PRENTON ROAD WEST

COW SHED STAND

AWAY

PITCH SIZE
110 X 70 yards

KOP STAND
(JOHN KING)

DISABLED
FANS

MAIN STAND

P (PERMIT HOLDERS ONLY)

# WALSALL

## Bescot Stadium, Bescot Crescent, Walsall, West Midlands, WS1 4SA

**Tel No:** 01922 622791
**Advance Tickets Tel No:** 01922 651416
**Fax:** 01922 613202
**Web Site:** http://www.saddlers.co.uk/
**E-Mail:** info@walsallfc.co.uk
**League:** 1st Division
**Brief History:** Founded 1888 as Walsall Town Swifts (amalgamation of Walsall Town – founded 1884 – and Walsall Swifts – founded 1885), changed name to Walsall in 1895. Former Grounds: The Chuckery, West Bromwich Road (twice), Hilary Street (later named Fellows Park, twice), moved to Bescot Stadium in 1990. Founder-members Second Division (1892). Record attendance 10,628 (25,343 at Fellows Park)
**(Total) Current Capacity:** 11,250 (10,500 seated) (prior to redevelopment)

**Visiting Supporters' Allocation:** 2,000 maximum in William Sharp Stand
**Club Colours:** Red shirts, red shorts
**Nearest Railway Station:** Bescot
**Parking (Car):** Car park at Ground
**Parking (Coach/Bus):** Car park at Ground
**Police Force and Tel No:** West Midlands (01922 638111)
**Disabled Visitors' Facilities:**
  **Wheelchairs:** Bank's Stand
  **Blind:** No special facility
**Anticipated Development(s):** The new two-tier Gilbert Allsop Stand was completed during the course of the 2002/03 season, taking the ground's capacity to 11,250. With its completion, away fans were transferred back to the William Sharp Stand. This completes planned development at the Bescot Stadium at present.

### KEY

**C** Club Offices
**S** Club Shop
**E** Entrance(s) for visiting supporters

↑ North direction (approx)

❶ Motorway M6
❷ M6 Junction 9
❸ Bescot BR Station
❹ Car Parks
❺ Bescot Crescent
❻ Gilbert Alsop Stand
❼ William Sharp Stand

*Above:* 695539; *Right:* 695531

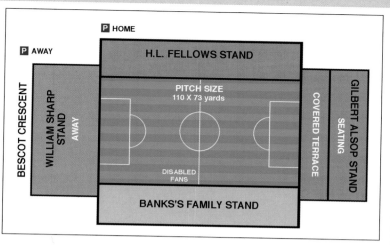

**P HOME**

**P AWAY**

BESCOT CRESCENT

P AWAY

H.L. FELLOWS STAND

WILLIAM SHARP STAND

AWAY

PITCH SIZE
110 X 73 yards

DISABLED FANS

COVERED TERRACE

GILBERT ALSOP STAND

SEATING

BANKS'S FAMILY STAND

Under experienced boss Colin Lee, who still has a year to run on his existing contract, the Saddlers were one of a numbers of teams that were never mathematically threatened with relegation but which hovered just above the First Division drop zone. Finishing in 17th place, on 54 points (eight above relegated Sheffield Wednesday), Lee's team also had the satisfaction, apart from guaranteeing themselves another season of First Division football, of looking down on ex-Premiership teams, Bradford, Coventry and Derby, all of which had struggled in the 2002/03 season. For 2003/04, it's hard to escape the conclusion that Walsall will again feature at the wrong end of the table, particularly as the threat from the promoted teams is stronger than usual.

# WATFORD

## Vicarage Road Stadium, Vicarage Road, Watford, WD18 0ER

**Tel No:** 01923 496000
**Advance Tickets Tel No:** 01923 496010
**Fax:** 01923 496001
**Web Site:** www.watfordfc.com
**E-Mail:** yourvoice@watfordfc.com
**League:** 1st Division
**Brief History:** Founded 1898 as an amalgamation of West Herts (founded 1891) and Watford St. Mary's (founded early 1890s). Former Grounds: Wiggenhall Road (Watford St. Mary's) and West Herts Sports Ground, moved to Vicarage Road in 1922. Founder-members Third Division (1920). Record attendance 34,099
**(Total) Current Capacity:** 22,100 (all seated)
**Visiting Supporters' Allocation:** 4,500 in Vicarage Road (North) Stand
**Club Colours:** Yellow shirts, red shorts
**Nearest Railway Station:** Watford High Street or Watford Junction

**Parking (Car):** Nearby multi-storey car park in town centre (10 mins walk)
**Parking (Coach/Bus):** Cardiff Road car park
**Police Force and Tel No:** Hertfordshire (01923 472000)
**Disabled Visitors' Facilities:**
  **Wheelchairs:** Corner East Stand and South Stand (special enclosure for approx. 24 wheelchairs), plus enclosure in North East Corner
  **Blind:** Commentary available in the East Stand (20 seats, free of charge)
**Anticipated Development(s):** Although the club announced plans for the reconstruction of the East Stand in order to provide 4,500 seats and increase Vicarage Road's capacity to 23,000, this work, which was due to start in 2002, has been put on ice temporarily whilst the financial consequences of the demise of ITV-Digital are counted.

### KEY

**C** Club Offices
**S** Club Shop

↑ North direction (approx)

❶ Vicarage Road
❷ Occupation Road
❸ Rous Stand
❹ Town Centre (¹/₂ mile) – Car Parks, High Street BR Station
❺ Vicarage Road Stand (away)
❻ East Stand
❼ Rookery End

*Above: 695969; Right: 695965*

Under Ray Lewington, the Hornets had a season of some success on the field, but like so many others were threatened by extinction off it. The club was one that sought (and got) the squad to agree to a deferment of pay, but there was and remains a real threat as a result of the compensation claim from ex-manager Gianluca Vialli. In the First Division, the team finished in mid-table, 13th with 60 points — never strong enough to make a sustained challenge for the Play-Offs but never sucked into the battle against relegation. The FA Cup, provided a high point, with the Hornets battling their way to the semi-final; unfortunately, Premiership outfit Southampton destroyed the romance of the cup, but the money thus generated from the run will still be useful in helping the club to balance its books. For 2003/04, it would again appear that the team has the potential to secure its First Division status with some ease, although another mid-table position come May 2004 is probably the best that can be hoped for.

# WEST BROMWICH ALBION

## The Hawthorns, Halfords Lane, West Bromwich, West Midlands, B71 4LF

**Tel No:** 0121 525 8888
**Advance Tickets Tel No:** 0121 525 8888
**Fax:** 0121 524 3462
**Web Site:** www.wba.co.uk
**E-Mail:** enquiries@wbafc.co.uk
**League:** 1st Division
**Brief History:** Founded 1879. Former Grounds: Coopers Hill, Dartmouth Park, Four Acres, Stoney Lane, moved to the Hawthorns in 1900. Founder-members of Football League (1888). Record attendance 64,815
**(Total) Current Capacity:** 28,000 (all seated)
**Visiting Supporters' Allocation:** 2,100
**Club Colours:** Navy blue and white striped shirts, white shorts
**Nearest Railway Station:** The Hawthorns

**Parking (Car):** Halfords Lane and Rainbow Stand car parks
**Parking (Coach/Bus):** Rainbow Stand car park
**Police Force and Tel No:** West Midlands (0121 554 3414)
**Disabled Visitors' Facilities:**
  **Wheelchairs:** Apollo 2000 and Smethwick Road End
  **Blind:** Facility available
**Anticipated Development(s):** There is speculation that the club will seek to increase capacity to 30,000 by rebuilding the area between the Apollo and East stands, but nothing is confirmed and the team's recent relegation may well reduce the immediate imperative to increase capacity.

---

*KEY*

**C** Club Offices
**S** Club Shop
**E** Entrance(s) for visiting supporters

⬆ North direction (approx)

❶ A41 Birmingham Road
❷ To M5 Junction 1
❸ Birmingham Centre (4 miles)
❹ Halfords Lane
❺ Main Stand
❻ Smethwick End
❼ Rolfe Street, Smethwick BR Station (1½ miles)
❽ To The Hawthorns BR Station
❾ East (Rainbow) Stand

*Above: 692739; Right: 692731*

Widely perceived by pundits and fans alike as relegation fodder, Gary Megson's Baggies lived up (or down) to expectations by making an immediate return to the First Division after a one-year sojourn in the Premiership. However, at least the team had the satisfaction of not finishing last — that dubious honour went to the toothless Black Cats — although in a normal season the Baggies' points total would have seen them finish in last place. Unlike promoted teams, West Brom did not go overboard in strengthening the squad with high-profile players on unrealistic salaries and will thus return to the First Division in a better position than many of the other relegated teams of recent years. Experience has shown, as with Leicester City, that it is possible for relegated teams to bounce straight back, but there is also the evidence of other teams that have failed to make an immediate return — such as Ipswich Town and Derby County — and, whilst the Baggies will be undoubtedly one of the favourites to make a promotion challenge, things might not be straightforward. Perhaps a Play-Off position at best?

# WEST HAM UNITED

## Boleyn Ground, Green Street, Upton Park, London, E13 9AZ

**Tel No:** 020 8548 2748
**Advance Tickets Tel No:** 020 8548 2700
**Fax:** 020 8548 2758
**Web Site:** http://www.whufc.co.uk
**League:** 1st Division
**Brief History:** Founded 1895 as Thames Ironworks, changed name to West Ham United in 1900. Former Grounds: Hermit Road, Browning Road, The Memorial Ground, moved to Boleyn Ground in 1904. Record attendance 42,322
**(Total) Current Capacity:** 35,647 (all seated)
**Visiting Supporters' Allocation:** 3,700 maximum
**Club Colours:** Claret and blue shirts, white shorts
**Nearest Railway Station:** Barking BR, Upton Park (tube)
**Parking (Car):** Street parking
**Parking (Coach/Bus):** As directed by Police

**Police Force and Tel No:** Metropolitan (020 8593 8232)
**Disabled Visitors' Facilities:**
  **Wheelchairs:** West Lower, Bobby Moore and Centenary Stands
  **Blind:** Commentaries available
**Anticipated Development(s):** The new 15,247-seat Dr Martens Stand opened in November 2001. The next phase of the ground's redevelopment will see the reconstruction of the East Stand. Although the club had plans to reconstruct the East Stand and extend both the Bobby Moore and Centenary stands, with a view to increasing the ground's capacity to 40,00, this work had been deferred as a result of relegation and the loss of income that playing in the First Division results in.

## KEY

**E** Entrance(s) for visiting supporters

↑ North direction (approx)

❶ A124 Barking Road
❷ Green Stree
❸ North Stand
❹ Upton Park Tube Station (¼ mile)
❺ Barking BR Station (1 mile)
❻ Bobby Moore Stand
❼ East Stand
❽ West Stand

*Above:* 692171; *Right:* 692169

There is one statistic in the Premiership that all clubs don't want: every team that has been last at Christmas has been relegated the following spring. In 2002/03 the club in that unenviable position was West Ham United. However, it was not until the last game of the season — with Trevor Brooking in temporary charge as a result of Glenn Roeder's hospitalisation towards the end of the campaign — that relegation was confirmed. Equal with Bolton Wanderers on points, but with an inferior goal difference, the Hammers needed to better Bolton's result in order to stay up. In the event, Bolton's victory over Middlesbrough made West Ham's draw with Birmingham City academic and First Division football will be the fare at Upton Park in 2003/04. Undoubtedly, the summer will see a number of high profile players, led probably by the mercurial Paolo di Canio, depart and there will also be speculation about the future management of the team. Will Roeder return when recovered from his health scare or will Brooking find an appetite for management in the long term? In any event, the Hammers should retain enough quality players to ensure that the team is one of the favourites for promotion. The loss of revenue will, however, be a major handicap.

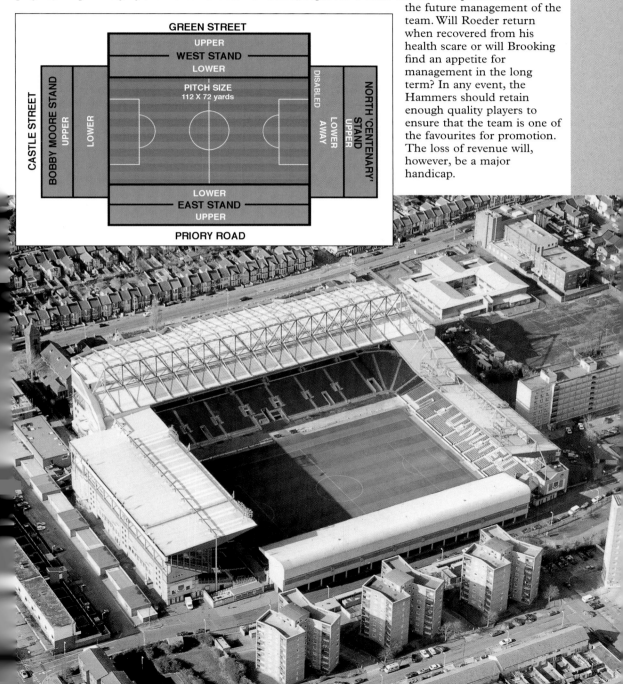

# WIGAN ATHLETIC

## JJB Stadium, Loire Drive, Robin Park, Wigan, Lancashire WN5 0UZ

**Tel No:** 01942 774000
**Advance Tickets Tel No:** 0870 112 2552
**Fax:** 01942 770466
**Web Site:** www.wiganlatics.co.uk
**E-Mail:** s.hayton@jjbstadium.co.uk
**League:** 1st Division
**Brief History:** Founded 1932. Springfield Park used by former Wigan Borough (Football League 1921-1931) but unrelated to current club. Elected to Football League in 1978 (the last club to be elected rather than promoted). Moved to JJB Stadium for start of 1999/2000 season. Record attendance at Springfield Park 27,500; at JJB Stadium 15,593
**(Total) Current Capacity:** 25,000 (all-seated)
**Visiting Supporters' Allocation:** 8,178 (maximum) in East Stand (all-seated)

**Club Colours:** White and blue shirts, blue shorts
**Nearest Railway Stations:** Wigan Wallgate/Wigan North Western (both about 1.5 miles away)
**Parking (Car):** 2,500 spaces at the ground
**Parking (Coach/Bus):** As directed
**Police Force and Tel No:** Greater Manchester (0161 872 5050)
**Disabled Visitors' Facilities**
  **Wheelchairs:** 100 spaces
  **Blind:** No special facility although it is hoped to have a system in place shortly
**Anticipated Development(s):** None following completion of the ground.

---

### KEY

**C** Club Offices
**E** Entrance(s) for visiting supporters

↑ North direction (approx)

❶ Loire Drive
❷ Anjoy Boulevard
❸ Car Parks
❹ Robin Park Arena
❺ River Douglas
❻ Leeds-Liverpool Canal
❼ To A577/A49 and Wigan town centre plus Wigan (Wallgate) and Wigan (North Western) station
❽ East Stand
❾ South Stand
❿ North Stand
● West Stand

*Above: 685070; Right: 685060*

Although Paul Jewell's first season at the JJB Stadium may not have proved a resounding success, the promotion from the Second Division achieved at the end of the 2002/03 season has shown that both Dave Whelan and the Wigan faithful were right to stand behind the manager. With the team storming through its league programme, losing only four times during the course of it and amassing 100 points, Athletic were undoubtedly the dominant force in the division. With Jewell's experience in taking Bradford City up to the Premiership in 1999, the club has a manager well capable of cementing the team's position at a higher level. Reunited with assistant Chris Hutchings, Jewell — who has just signed a new three-year extension to his contract — looks capable of building a team that seems as though it could prosper in the First Division. Teams recently promoted from the Second Division, such as Millwall and Reading, have all performed well at this level and, given Whelan's backing, Wigan has the potential to be as successful. There is every possibility that the team could feature in the Play-Offs: Wigan in the Premiership — now that's a dream that would inspire most lower division chairmen and managers.

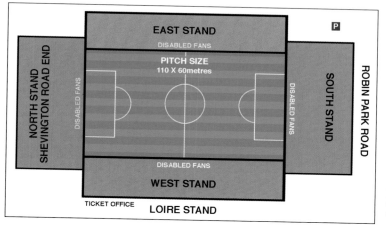

# WIMBLEDON

## National Hockey Stadium, Silbury Boulevard, Milton Keynes, MK9 1HA

**Tel No:** 020 8771 2233*
**Advance Tickets Tel No:** 020 8771 8841*
**Fax:** 020 8768 0641*
* Note these are the numbers for Wimbledon whilst at Selhurst Park and will no doubt change with the club's relocation.
**National Hockey Stadium:** 01908 246800
**Web Site:** www.wimbledon-fc.co.uk
**League:** 1st Division
**Brief History:** Founded 1889 at Wimbledon Old Centrals, changed name to Wimbledon in 1905. Former grounds: Wimbledon Common, Pepy's Road, Grand Drive, Merton Hall Road, Malden Wanderers Cricket Ground, Plough Lane and moved to Selhurst Park in 1991. Probable move to National Hockey Stadium 2002. Elected to Football League in 1977. Record attendance (Plough Lane) 18,000; (Selhurst Park) 30,115.
**(Total) Current Capacity:** tbc
**Visiting Supporters' Allocation:** To be confirmed
**Club Colours:** Blue shirts, blue shorts
**Nearest Railway Station:** Milton Keynes Central
**Parking (Car):** At ground
**Parking (Coach/Bus):** As directed

**Police Force and Tel No:** Thames Valley Police (01865 846000)
**Disabled Visitors' Facilities:**
  **Wheelchairs:** tbc
  **Blind:** tbc
**Anticipated Development(s):** After some years of uncertainty as to the club's future location, the move to Milton Keynes has been sanctioned and the club will possibly start the 2003/04 season at a temporary home at the National Hockey Stadium whilst a new permanent ground is constructed at Denbigh. It is expected that the new 28,000 all-seater stadium will be completed for the start of the 2007/08 season at the latest (the Dons were granted final permission to move by the Football League in April 2003 on the basis that the new ground would be available no later than June 2007). Now that as the club has gone into Administration and no work has been undertaken on the upgrading of the National Hockey Stadium, it is possible that the club's first 'home' fixtures will be at Selhurst Park. If that is the case, please refer to the Crystal Palace entry for details.

| KEY | |
|---|---|
| ↑ | North direction (approx) |
| ❶ | National Hockey Stadium |
| ❷ | Milton Keynes Central station |
| ❸ | Grafton Gate |
| ❹ | A509 Portway |
| ❺ | A509 Portway to A5 junction |
| ❻ | Silbury Boulevard |
| ❼ | To town centre |

Wimbledon's last season at Selhurst Park before the controversial move to Milton Keynes was marked by a sorry procession of abysmal crowds as many of the Crazy Gang's traditional supporters boycotted 'Franchise FC' in favour of the newly formed AFC Wimbledon. *The Independent* newspaper on a Monday had a regular column called 'A Tale of Two Dons' which recorded the on- and off-field activities of both teams, with the new non-league team regularly outstripping the First Division team in terms of support. For the relatively small Selhurst Park band of supporters, the campaign in 2002/03 started slowly as Stuart Murdoch's team, perhaps overshadowed by the controversy, took time to get going in the First Division, but a dramatic improvement in form in the second half of the season saw the team at one stage threaten a Play-Off berth. Finishing in 10th place, nine points below Forest in sixth, is probably a good foundation for the new season, although it will be interesting to see how many of those that have supported Wimbledon through the past season will make the trip up the M1 if the team fails to perform adequately. Difficult to forecast: the Dons could easily head out of the First Division in either direction depending on how well or badly they start the year.

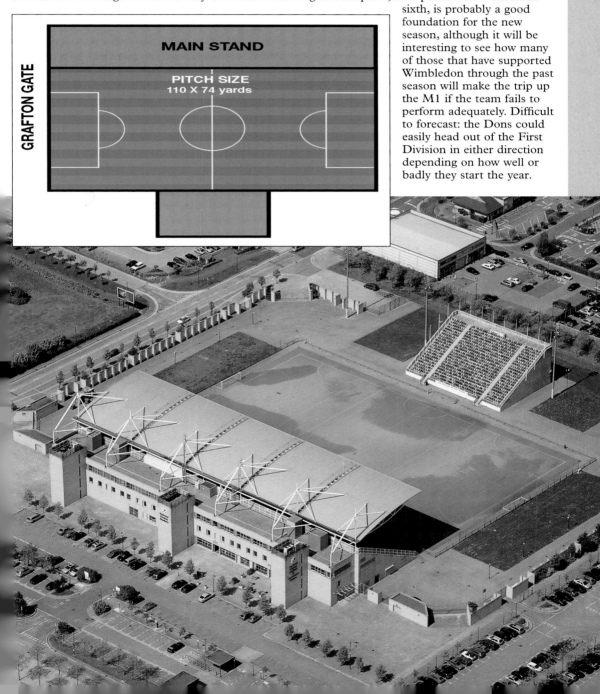

GRAFTON GATE

MAIN STAND

PITCH SIZE
110 X 74 yards

# WOLVERHAMPTON WANDERERS

## Molineux Ground, Waterloo Road, Wolverhampton, WV1 4QR

**Tel No:** 01902 655000
**Advance Tickets Tel No:** 01902 653653
**Fax:** 01902 687006
**Web Site:** www.wolves.co.uk
**E-Mail:** info@wolves.co.uk
**League:** F.A. Premiership
**Brief History:** Founded 1877 as St. Lukes, combined with Goldthorn Hill to become Wolverhampton Wanderers in 1884. Former Grounds: Old Windmill Field, John Harper's Field and Dudley Road, moved to Molineux in 1889. Founder-members Football League (1888). Record attendance 61,315
**(Total) Current Capacity:** 28,525 (all seated)

**Visiting Supporters' Allocation:** 1,500 in Jack Harris Stand or 2,971 in lower tier of John Ireland Stand
**Club Colours:** Gold shirts, black shorts
**Nearest Railway Station:** Wolverhampton
**Parking (Car):** West Park and adjacent North Bank
**Parking (Coach/Bus):** As directed by Police
**Police Force and Tel No:** West Midlands (01902 649000)
**Disabled Visitors' Facilities:**
 **Wheelchairs:** 104 places on two sides
 **Blind:** Commentary (by prior arrangement)

## KEY

**C** Club Offices
**S** Club Shop
**E** Entrance(s) for visiting supporters
**R** Refreshment bars for visiting supporters
**T** Toilets for visiting supporters

⬆ North direction (approx)

❶ Stan Cullis Stand
❷ John Ireland Stand
❸ Billy Wright Stand
❹ Ring Road – St. Peters
❺ Waterloo Road
❻ A449 Stafford Street
❼ BR Station (1/2 mile)
❽ Jack Harris Stand
❾ Molineux Street
❿ Molineux Way

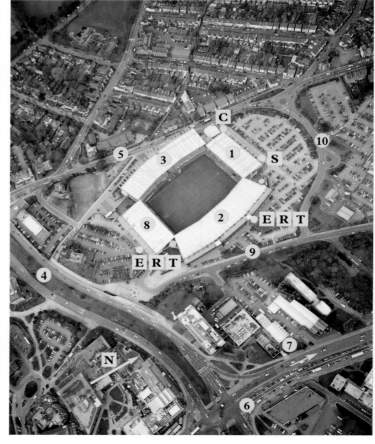

*Above:* 691712; *Right:* 691706

One of the undoubted fallen giants of English football, Wolves had spent almost two decades outside the top division at the start of the 2002/03 campaign and rumours were rife that failure to make progress in this campaign would lead both to the departure of Dave Jones as manager and the reduction of Sir Jack Hayward's investment in the team. Whilst never being good enough to mount a serious challenge to Leicester and Portsmouth, Wolves ultimately finished the season in fifth place and were, therefore, guaranteed a place in the Play-Offs. Victory in the semi-final over Reading took the team to the Play-Off final at the Millennium Stadium against much fancied Sheffield United. A stunning first half display, in which three goals were scored, ensured Wolves' victory and with it promotion to the Premiership. However, as the team promoted through the Play-Offs, Wolves are already widely perceived as amongst the bookies' favourites for relegation. On their day Wolves have proved that they can live with the best — witness their victory over Newcastle in the FA Cup in 2002/03 — but the feeling must be that there will be too few of these days to ensure Premiership survival.

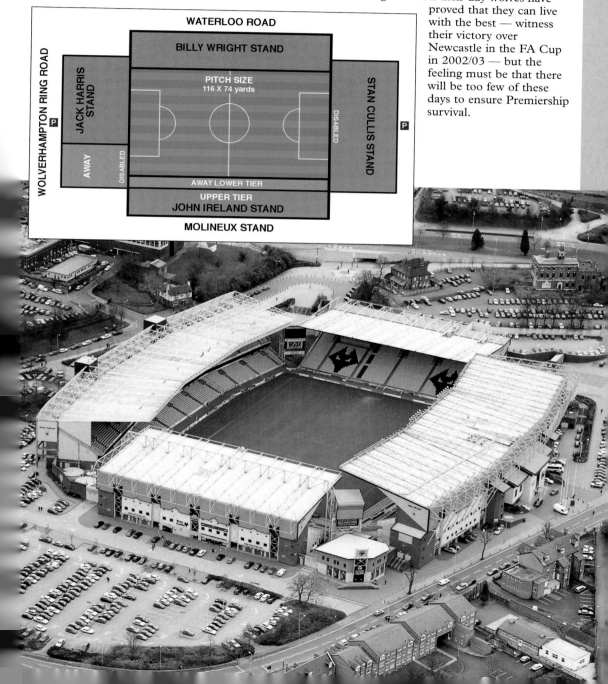

WATERLOO ROAD

BILLY WRIGHT STAND

WOLVERHAMPTON RING ROAD

JACK HARRIS STAND

AWAY

DISABLED

PITCH SIZE
116 X 74 yards

STAN CULLIS STAND

DISABLED

AWAY LOWER TIER
UPPER TIER
JOHN IRELAND STAND

MOLINEUX STAND

# WREXHAM

## Racecourse Ground, Mold Road, Wrexham, Clwyd LL11 2AH

**Tel No:** 01978 262129
**Advance Tickets Tel No:** 01978 262129
**Web Site:** www.wrexhamafc.co.uk
**E-Mail:** wrexhamfootballclub@hotmail.com
**Fax:** 01978 357821
**League:** 2nd Division
**Brief History:** Founded 1873 (oldest Football Club in Wales). Former Ground: Acton Park, permanent move to Racecourse Ground c.1900. Founder-members Third Division North (1921). Record attendance 34,445
**(Total) Current Capacity:** 15,500 (11,500 seated)
**Visiting Supporters' Allocation:** 3,100 (maximum; all seated)

**Club Colours:** Red shirts, white shorts
**Nearest Railway Station:** Wrexham General
**Parking (Car):** (Nearby) Town car parks
**Parking (Coach/Bus):** As directed by Police
**Police Force and Tel No:** Wrexham Division (01978 290222)
**Disabled Visitors' Facilities:**
  **Wheelchairs:** Pryce Griffiths Stand
  **Blind:** No special facility
**Anticipated Development(s):** Following completion of the Pryce Griffiths Stand, attention will next turn to the Kop End Terrace. However, this will be retained as terracing for as long as possible and there will be no change in the immediate future.

### KEY

**C** Club Offices
**S** Club Shop
**E** Entrance(s) for visiting supporters
**R** Refreshment bars for visiting supporters
**T** Toilets for visiting supporters

⬆ North direction (approx)

❶ Wrexham General Station
❷ A541 – Mold Road
❸ Wrexham Town Centre
❹ Pryce Griffiths Stand
❺ Kop Town End
❻ To Wrexham Central Station

*Above:* 685071; *Right:* 685072

After the disappointment of joining the Nationwide League's basement division at the end of 2001/02, last season was one of considerable success for Denis Smith's team, with promotion back to the Second Division being achieved at the first attempt. Finishing third, behind Rushden and Hartlepool, some 10 points above the Play-Off zone means that the new season will see Second Division football at the Racecourse Ground. However, as with all promoted teams, there will

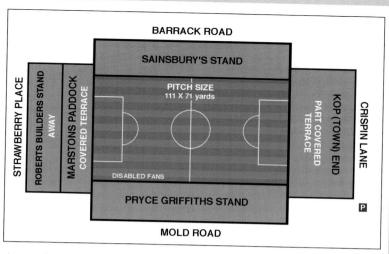

need to be a period of consolidation at the start of the new campaign or there could be a very real threat that the team will struggle to maintain itself at this level.

# WYCOMBE WANDERERS

## Adams Park, Hillbottom Road, Sands, High Wycombe, Bucks HP12 4HJ

**Tel No:** 01494 472100
**Advance Tickets Tel No:** 01494 441118
**Fax:** 01494 527633
**Web Site:** wycombewanderers.co.uk
**E-Mail:** wwfc@wycombewanderers.co.uk
**League:** 2nd Division
**Brief History:** Founded 1884. Former Grounds: The Rye, Spring Meadows, Loakes Park, moved to Adams Park 1990. Promoted to Football League 1993. Record attendance 15,678 (Loakes Park); 9,921 (Adams Park)
**(Total) Current Capacity:** 10,000 (8,250 seated)
**Visiting Supporters' Allocation:** c2,000 in the Roger Vere Stand
**Club Colours:** Sky blue with navy blue quartered shirts, blue shorts

**Nearest Railway Station:** High Wycombe (2¹/₂ miles)
**Parking (Car):** At Ground and Street parking
**Parking (Coach/Bus):** At Ground
**Police Force and Tel No:** Thames Valley (01494 465888)
**Disabled Visitors' Facilities:**
  **Wheelchairs:** Special shelter – Main Stand, Hillbottom Road end
  **Blind:** Commentary available
**Anticipated Development(s):** With the completion of the new 2,000-seat Roger Vere Stand there is no further work currently planned.

---

### KEY

**C** Club Offices
**S** Club Shop
**E** Entrance(s) for visiting supporters

↑ North direction (approx)

❶ Car Park
❷ Hillbottom Road (Industrial Estate)
❸ M40 Junction 4 (approx 2 miles)
❹ Wycombe Town Centre (approx 2¹/₂ miles)
❺ Servispak Stand
❻ Roger Vere Stand (away)

*Above:* 692830; *Right:* 692818

For a couple of seasons it appeared that Lawrie Sanchez, aided by the high profile cup campaign in 2000/01, could do little wrong with Wycombe, but the failure of the team to impress in the Second Division in 2002/03, heightened by failure in the two cup competitions, has seen elements within the Adams Park faithful turn against him. The 2002/03 campaign in the Second Division was marked by the real threat that the team would get sucked into the relegation battle, although the team ultimately finished in 17th position some six points off the drop. The new season could, however, spell disaster for Sanchez unless the squad's performances improve. If the club is again drawn towards the bottom half of the table it could well be that Wanderers ends the season with a new man in the managerial hot seat.

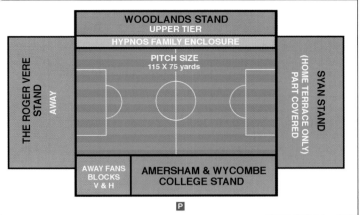

WOODLANDS STAND
UPPER TIER

HYPNOS FAMILY ENCLOSURE

PITCH SIZE
115 X 75 yards

THE ROGER VERE STAND

AWAY

SYAN STAND
(HOME TERRACE ONLY)
PART COVERED

AWAY FANS BLOCKS V & H

AMERSHAM & WYCOMBE COLLEGE STAND

P

# YEOVIL TOWN

## Huish Park, Lufton Way, Yeovil, Somerset BA22 8YF

**Tel No:** 01935 423662
**Advance Tickets Tel No:** 01935 423662
**Fax:** 01935 473956
**Web Site:** www.ytfc.net
**League** 3rd Division
**Brief History:** Founded as Yeovil Casuals in 1895 and merged with Petters United in 1920. Moved to old ground (Huish) in 1920 and relocated to Huish Park in 1990. Founder members of Alliance Premier League in 1979 but relegated in 1985. Returned to Premier League in 1988 but again relegated in 1996. Promoted to the now retitled Conference in 1997 and promoted to the Nationwide League in 2003. Record Attendance: (at Huish) 16,318 (at Huish Park) 8868
**(Total) Current Capacity:** 9,100 (5,212 seated)

**Visiting Supporters' Allocation:** 1,700 on Copse Road Terrace (open) plus c400 seats in Bartlett Stand.
**Club Colours:** Green shirts, white shorts
**Nearest Railway Station:** Yeovil Junction or Yeovil Pen Mill
**Parking (Car):** Car park near to stadium for 800 cars
**Parking (Coach/Bus):** As directed
**Police Force and Tel No:** Avon & Somerset (01935 415291)
**Disabled Visitors' Facilities:**
 **Wheelchairs:** Up to 20 dedicated located in the Bartlett Stand
 **Blind:** No special facility

---

### KEY

⬆ North direction (approx)

❶ Western Avenue
❷ Copse Road
❸ Lufton Way
❹ Artillery Road
❺ Main Stand
❻ Bartlett Stand
❼ Westland Stand
❽ Copse Road Terrace (away)
❾ Memorial Road
❿ Mead Avenue
⬤ To town centre (one mile) and stations (two to four miles)

*Above:* 695579; *Right:* 695573

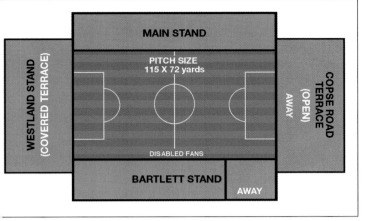

**MAIN STAND**

**PITCH SIZE**
115 X 72 yards

**WESTLAND STAND (COVERED TERRACE)**

**COPSE ROAD TERRACE (OPEN) AWAY**

DISABLED FANS

**BARTLETT STAND**

**AWAY**

Following a number of near misses in recent seasons, one of the great names of non-league football finally joined the Nationwide League at the end of the 2002/03 season. Yeovil Town, a club immortalised for ever as a result of its legendary cup upsets from the past, dominated the Conference right from the start and it came as no surprise that the team secured promotion with a storming victory away at promotion rivals Doncaster Rovers in a match televised live by Sky. Under Gary Johnson, the Glovers will be keen to become a force in the 3rd Division, although, as with other promoted teams, there is always the possibility, as Boston United discovered, that a leap up the league structure cannot always easily be successful. With Yeovil's promotion, League football arrives in Somerset for the first time, along with the realisation that Town can no longer be regarded as one of minnows — the ironic thing will be to see the results of the club's first exploits as a League team in the FA Cup!

# YORK CITY

## Bootham Crescent, York, YO30 7AQ

**Tel No:** 01904 624447
**Advance Tickets Tel No:** 01904 624447
**Fax:** 01904 631457
**Web Site:** www.ycfc.net
**E-mail:** cityreds@virgin.net
**League:** 3rd Division
**Brief History:** Founded 1922. Former ground: Fulfordgate Ground, moved to Bootham Crescent in 1932. Record attendance 28,123
**(Total) Current Capacity:** 9,034 (3,509 seated)
**Visiting Supporters' Allocation:** 2,380 (336 seated)
**Club Colours:** Red shirts, blue shorts

**Nearest Railway Station:** York
**Parking (Car):** Street parking
**Parking (Coach/Bus):** As directed by Police
**Police Force and Tel No:** North Yorkshire (01904 631321)
**Disabled Visitors' Facilities:**
  **Wheelchairs:** In front of Family Stand
  **Blind:** Commentary available
**Anticipated Development(s):** The club has long term plans to relocate, although nothing is confirmed at present. Expect the team to remain at Bootham Crescent for at least one season.

### KEY

**C** Club Offices
**S** Club Shop
**E** Entrance(s) for visiting supporters
**R** Refreshment bars for visiting supporters
**T** Toilets for visiting supporters

↑ North direction (approx)

❶ Bootham Crescent
❷ Grosvenor Road
❸ Burton Stone Lane
❹ York BR Station (1 mile)

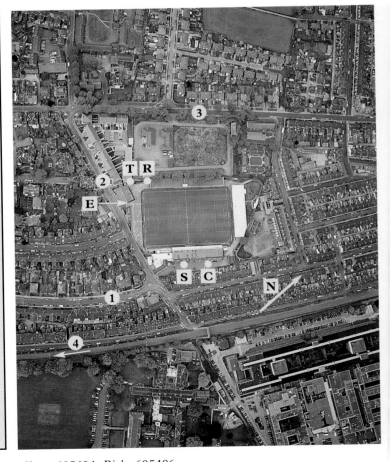

*Above:* 695494; *Right:* 695486

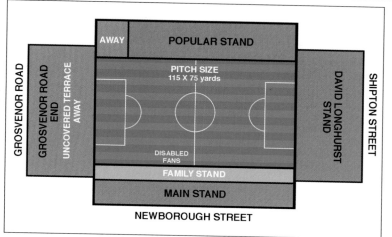

One of a number of teams whose existence was under threat during much of the season, it seemed a very real possibility that York City would fold during the early part of 2003. In the event the club survived and is now under the control of a supporters' trust, an organisation that undertook considerable fund raising activities during the year in order to keep the club afloat. Although overshadowed to a considerable extent by events off the field, the Minstermen performed well under Terry Dolan's management and it seemed likely at one stage that the team would make the Play-Offs. In the event, however, results towards the end of the season meant that City finished in 10th place. Towards the end of May, Dolan was sacked, the implication being that it was a financial rather than a footballing concern resulting in his departure. With the new manager, Chris Brass, uncertain about the size and strength of his squad for 2003/04 the suspicion must be that York will struggle in the forthcoming season.

# WEMBLEY

## Wembley Stadium, Wembley HA9 0DW

**Tel No:** tbc
**Advance Tickets Tel No:** tbc
**Fax:** tbc
**Brief History:** Inaugurated for FA Cup Final of 1923, venue for many major national and international matches including the World Cup Final of 1966. Also traditionally used for other major sporting events and as a venue for rock concerts and other entertainments. Last used prior to redevelopment as a football ground versus Germany in October 2001. Ground subsequently demolished during late 2002.
**(Total) Current Capacity:** tbc
**Nearest Railway Station:** Wembley Complex (National Rail), Wembley Central (National Rail and London Underground), Wembley Park (London Underground)

**Parking (Car):** Limited parking at ground and nearby
**Parking (Coach Bus):** As advised by police
**Police Force:** Metropolitan
**Disabled Facilities**
  **Wheelchairs:** tbc
  **Blind:** tbc
**Anticipated Development(s):** After several years of dithering and following the final game played at the 'old' Wembley, demolition of the old ground was completed in late 2002 and work started on the construction of the new stadium. This is scheduled for completion in 2006.

KEY

*Above:* 695982